LONDON

THE SECRET ATLAS

Rachel Howard and Bill Nash

PHOTOGRAPHS

Stéphanie Rivoal, Jorge Monedero and Adam Tucker

JONGLEZ PUBLISHING

We have taken great pleasure in drawing up *London – The Secret Atlas* and hope that through its guidance you will, like us, continue to discover unusual, hidden or little-known aspects of the city.

Descriptions of certain places are accompanied by thematic sections highlighting historical details or anecdotes as an aid to understanding the city in all its complexity.

This atlas also draws attention to the multitude of details found in places that we may pass every day without noticing.

It is an invitation to look more closely at the urban landscape and, more generally, a means of seeing our own city with the curiosity and attention that we often display while travelling elsewhere …

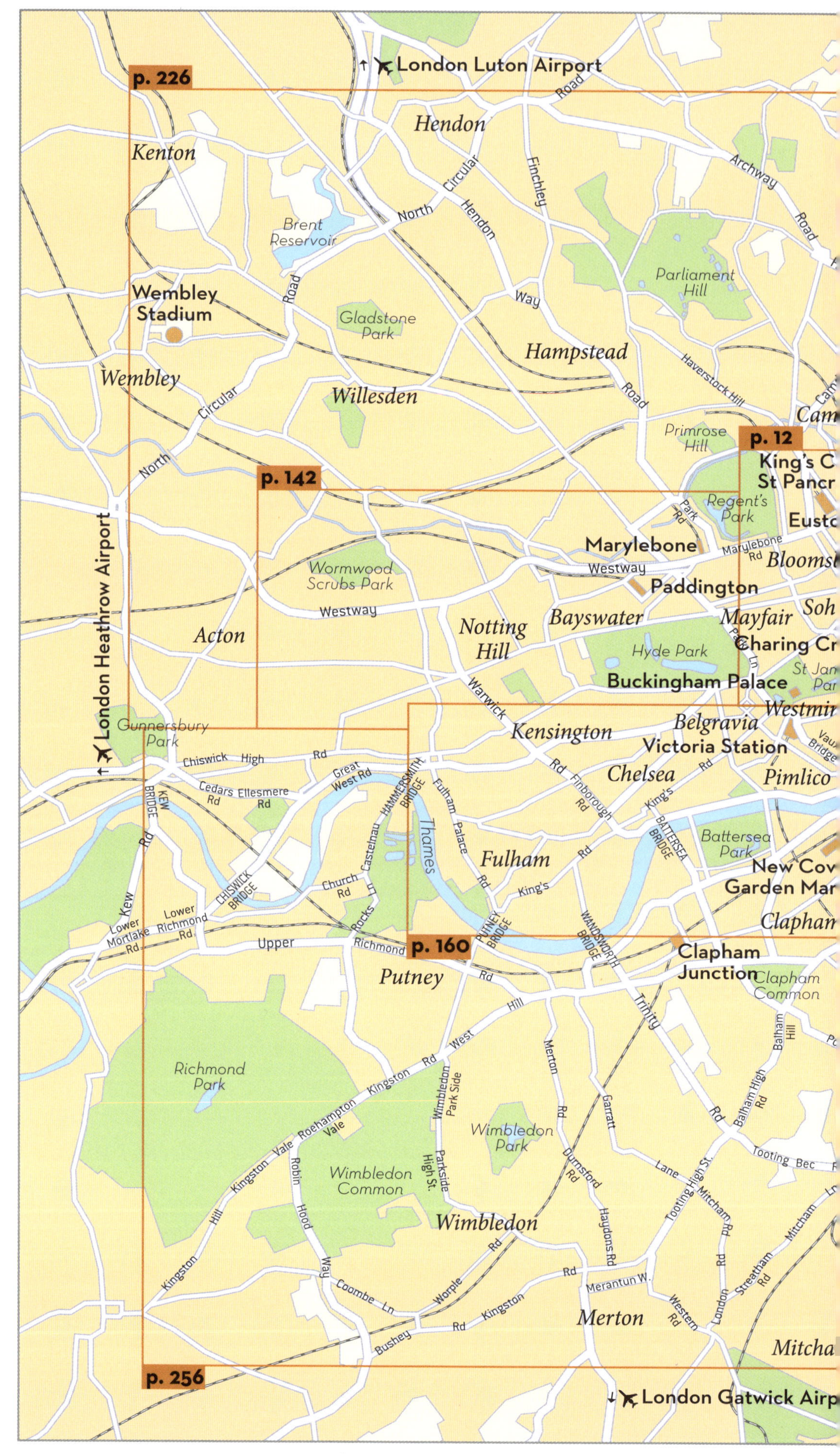

London Luton Airport
p. 226
Hendon
Kenton
Brent Reservoir
North Circular
Finchley
Hendon Way
Archway Road
Parliament Hill
Wembley Stadium
Gladstone Park
Hampstead
Haverstock Hill
Road
Wembley
Willesden
Circular
North
Primrose Hill
p. 12
King's C
St Pancr
p. 142
Regent's Park
Park Rd
Eusto
London Heathrow Airport
Marylebone
Marylebone Rd
Bloomsb
Westway
Wormwood Scrubs Park
Paddington
Westway
Acton
Notting Hill
Bayswater
Mayfair
Soh
Hyde Park
Park Ln
Charing Cr
St Jam Par
Buckingham Palace
Westmin
Warwick
Gunnersbury Park
Kensington
Belgravia
Victoria Station
Chiswick High Rd
Great West Rd
Cedars Rd
Ellesmere Rd
HAMMERSMITH BRIDGE
Chelsea
Pimlico
KEW BRIDGE
Fulham Palace Rd
Finborough Rd
King's Rd
BATTERSEA BRIDGE
Thames
Battersea Park
Castelnau
Fulham
New Cov Garden Mar
Church Rd
King's
Kew Rd
CHISWICK BRIDGE
Lower Richmond Rd
Rocks Ln
Clapham
Lower Mortlake Rd
Upper Richmond Rd
p. 160
PUTNEY BRIDGE
WANDSWORTH BRIDGE
Clapham Junction
Putney
Rd
Clapham Common
Hill
West
Trinity Rd
Balham Hill
Richmond Park
Kingston Rd
Merton Rd
Garratt Lane
Roehampton Vale
Wimbledon Park Side
Wimbledon Park
Balham High Rd
Kingston Vale
Robin Hood Way
Wimbledon Common
Parkside
High St.
Durnsford Rd
Tooting Bec
Tooting High St.
Mitcham Rd
Wimbledon
Haydons Rd
Kingston Hill
Worple Rd
Merantun W.
Rd
Streatham Rd
London Rd
Mitcham Ln
Coombe Ln
Western Rd
Kingston Rd
Merton
Bushey Rd
Mitcha
p. 256
London Gatwick Airp

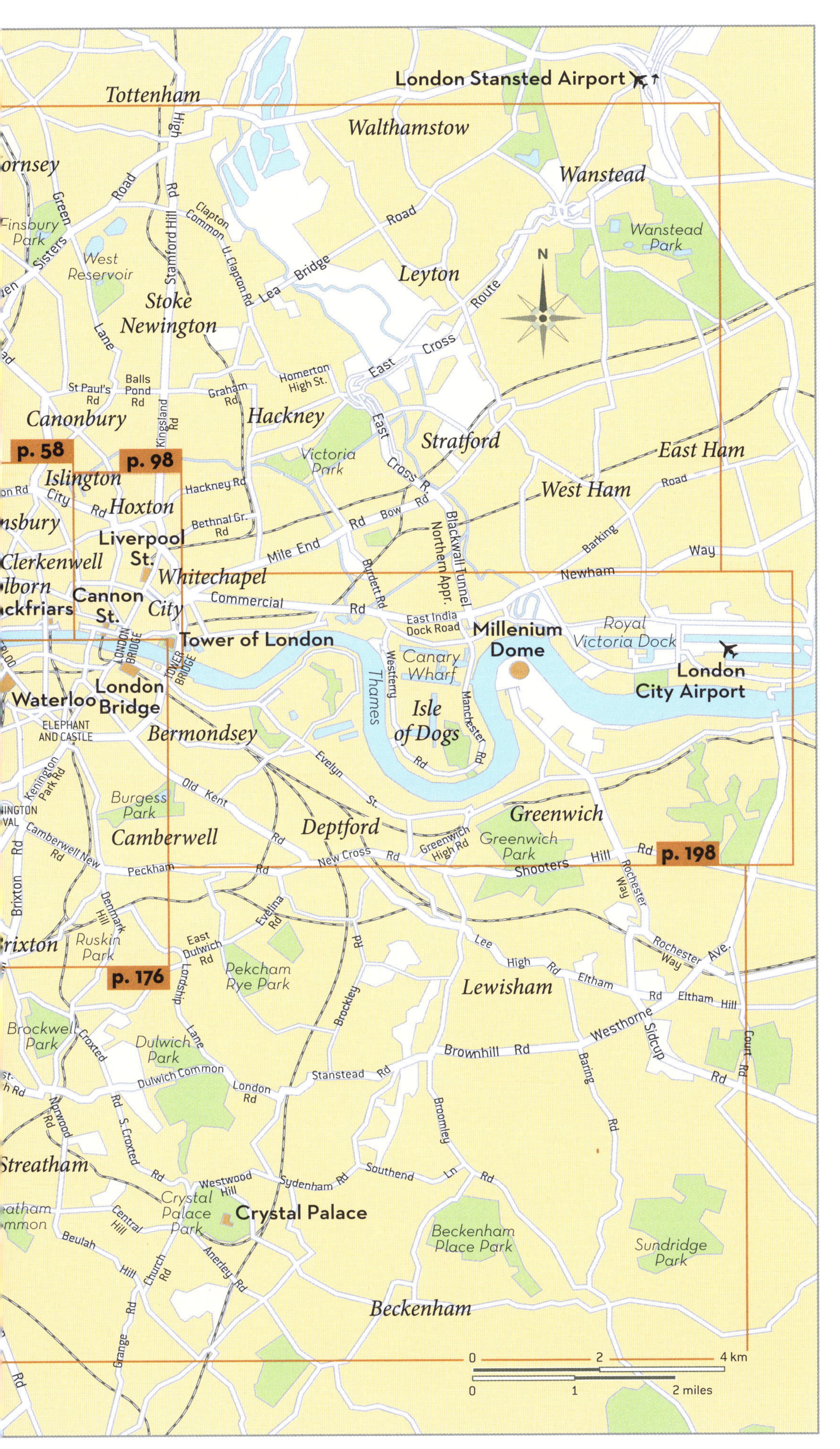

London Stansted Airport
Tottenham
Walthamstow
Wanstead
Wanstead Park
Leyton
Stoke Newington
West Reservoir
Finsbury Park
Canonbury
Hackney
Victoria Park
Stratford
East Ham
West Ham
p. 58
p. 98
Islington
Hoxton
Liverpool St.
Clerkenwell
Whitechapel
Cannon St.
City
Tower of London
Millenium Dome
Royal Victoria Dock
London City Airport
Canary Wharf
Isle of Dogs
Thames
London Bridge
Waterloo
Bermondsey
Elephant and Castle
Burgess Park
Camberwell
Deptford
Greenwich
Greenwich Park
p. 198
p. 176
Ruskin Park
Pekcham Rye Park
Lewisham
Brockwell Park
Dulwich Park
Streatham
Crystal Palace Park
Crystal Palace
Beckenham Place Park
Sundridge Park
Beckenham
0 2 4 km
0 1 2 miles

WESTMINSTER TO CAMDEN

ANGEL TO TEMPLE

SHOREDITCH TO TOWER BRIDGE

SHEPHERD'S BUSH TO MARYLEBONE

HAMMERSMITH TO WESTMINSTER

SOUTH BANK TO BRIXTON

WHITECHAPEL TO WOOLWICH

GREATER LONDON (NORTH)

GREATER LONDON (SOUTH)

CAMDEN
SOMERS TOWN
King's Cross
St Pancras
King's Cross St Pancras
Euston
REGENT'S PARK
Regent's Park
Mornington Crescent
Euston Square
University College
Great Portland Street
Warren Street
Marylebone
Regent's Park
ST PANCRAS
Coram's Fields
Russell Square
BLOOMSBURY
British Museum
Goodge
Tottenham Court Road
Holborn
Oxford Circus
Bond Street
SOHO
Covent Garden
Royal Opera House
COVENT GARDEN
Leicester Square
Royal Academy of Arts
Piccadilly Circus
National Gallery
Charing Cross
Embankment
Green Park
Hyde Park Corner
St James's Park
Buckingham Palace
Palace Gardens
WESTMINSTER
Westminster
St James's Park
Westminster Abbey
BELGRAVIA
Thames

WESTMINSTER TO CAMDEN

01.

Old St Pancras Churchyard, Pancras Road, NW1 1UL
King's Cross St Pancras tube/rail, Mornington Crescent tube

REMAINS OF THE HARDY TREE

Rearranging the dead

Famously gloomy 19th-century novelist Thomas Hardy may have had his distaste for the city confirmed by his involvement with this North London oddity. Hardy trained as an architect at King's College, and was apprenticed to Arthur Blomfield between 1862 and 1867, a time when railway networks in the UK were expanding rapidly. Blomfield was commissioned by the Bishop of London to supervise the exhumation of human remains and the dismantling of tombs in the churchyard at Old St Pancras to make way for the extension of the Midland Railway to its new terminus at King's Cross. Blomfield passed the job on to Hardy. Hardy must have spent hours in the churchyard helping to oversee the removal of bodies and tombs from the land designated for the new railway. He would have been 25 when he took on the job. It must have made a deep impression on him – certainly, progress riding roughshod over tradition is a recurrent theme in his books.

The Victorians were obsessed by death and made a fetish of all its trappings. They had a particular horror of cremation, so the preservation of the physical remains of the dead was extremely important to them. The headstones carried less meaning for the Victorians than the corpses, and in most cases would have simply been discarded. However, some were stacked in a tightly packed circle around this ash tree. Over the years, the tree has grown around them and the mossy headstones are beginning to become part of it; they now look like a strange crop. What remains is an accidental and effective memento mori, which almost certainly inspired Hardy's poem, 'The Levelled Churchyard':

We late-lamented, resting here,
Are mixed to human jam,
And each to each exclaims in fear,
'I know not which I am!'

The original tree fell, leaving only a hole surrounded by graves. In 2024, the foundation decided to replant a tree further away. The graves remained in their original position and the tree was felled. Its trunks have been transformed into a kind of seat that can now be admired.

OLD ST PANCRAS GRAVEYARD

Charles Dickens describes Old St Pancras graveyard in 'A Tale of Two Cities' as a sinister place where body snatchers used to 'fish'. Sir John Soane is among those buried in the churchyard, in a surprisingly understated (for him) tomb that provided the inspiration for Sir Giles Gilbert Scott's iconic red telephone boxes. Mary Wollstonecraft and William Godwin were originally buried here (there is a monument to her in the churchyard), though her remains now lie in Bournemouth. Wollstonecraft's daughter, Mary, author of Frankenstein, supposedly planned her elopement with the poet Shelley during clandestine meetings at her mother's grave.

02.

Keystone Cres
Kings Cross St Pancras tube

KEYSTONE CRESCENT

The smallest crescent in Europe

The area around Kings Cross station is generally busy, overcrowded and dirty. But buried in the heart of this bustling district is a tiny row of charming 19th-century houses that make up the smallest crescent in Europe: Keystone Crescent is a uniform row of 24 houses in varying shades of brick that sweeps around into a curved semicircle.

This little street was built in 1864 by Robert James Stuckey, who learnt the bricklaying trade from his father and wanted to make the most out of the unusually shaped land. The houses are so tightly bound together that the road's radius is the tiniest in Europe (although the actual measurement is unknown). There have been a few attempts to demolish the street over the decades but luckily the area is now Grade II listed. Its traditional charm is protected by the local council, which has special regulations to keep the crescent as it was when first built. There are rules, for example, about the front gates: they must be replaced with traditional metal gates when they need repairing, and where possible they must be painted black. All houses must have slate roofs, a four-panelled door and obey a zero-tolerance policy on car ports.

Signs attached to the walls at each end of the street explain that it was originally called Caledonian Crescent (a faded old sign around the corner also attests to this). Stuckey named the road after the Caledonian Asylum, a nearby orphanage set up to look after Scottish children whose parents had died in the Napoleonic wars. Eventually the asylum was demolished and the road's name changed to Keystone, thought to be linked to the Masonic symbol of the Keystone.

For Sale

03.

St Pancras Church, Euston Road, NW1 2BA
Euston or King's Cross tube/rail

THE COADE STONE CARYATIDS

Maidens without midriffs

When it was built in 1819 for a whopping £89,296, St Pancras Church was the most expensive house of worship since the reconstruction of St Paul's Cathedral. Modelled on the Erechtheum of the Acropolis, the church's exterior has lost much of its lustre thanks to the traffic hurtling down Euston Road, one of London's least lovely thoroughfares. But the striking façade of caryatids that prop up the porch still turns heads.

On closer inspection, these maidens are stumpier than their Greek counterparts (one of whom is on display in the British Museum, courtesy of Lord Elgin). Sculptor Charles Rossi (1762–1839) spent almost three years crafting the caryatids out of Coade stone, an artificial material much favoured for the neoclassical monuments so popular in the 18th and early 19th centuries. The figures were built up in sections around cast-iron columns. But when Rossi transported them from his studio to the church, he discovered to his horror that the statues were too tall. Under the gaze of a bemused crowd of onlookers, Rossi took drastic action: he cut out their midriffs. Thankfully, their draped Grecian gowns help to conceal their stunted torsos.

The church hosts free recitals every Thursday afternoon, and exhibitions and concerts in the Crypt Gallery (cryptgallery.org).

Five hundred and fifty seven people lay buried in these underground vaults, which were used as an air raid shelter during WWII.

WHAT IS COADE STONE?

Founded by Mrs Eleanor Coade in 1769, Coade's Artificial Stone Manufactory dominated London's trade in statues, busts, tombstones, architectural and garden ornaments for almost 65 years.

Cheap, easy to mould and weather-resistant, Coade stone was made to a secret formula.

According to an anonymous account from 1806: 'It is possessed of the peculiar property of resisting frost, and consequently it retains its sharpness in which it excels every species of stone, and even equals marble'.

This quality is evident in the many Coade stone monuments scattered around London, notably Captain Bligh's tomb in St Mary's Lambeth, Nelson's pediment at the Royal Naval College Chapel in Greenwich, and the 13-ton lion on Westminster Bridge, one of a pair of that once crowned the Red Lion brewery on the South Bank.

The other lion guards the All-England Rugby Club at Twickenham, near the Rowland Hill Memorial Gate. Despite this success, the company went bankrupt not long after Eleanor Coade's death in 1796 at the grand old age of 88. She is buried in Bunhill Fields.

04.

12 Stephenson Way, NW1 2HD
Euston tube/rail, Euston Square tube

MAGIC CIRCLE MUSEUM

Abracadabra

First of all, get one thing straight – the only way you're getting into this museum is if you buy a ticket for one of the Magic Circle's public events, most of which are magic shows in the upstairs theatre. Don't turn up at HQ, knock on the door and expect to be welcomed – it drives the magicians crazy and they'll probably saw you in half. Anyway, the shows feature some of the best magicians in Britain and are well worth the entrance fee.

Once you've found the place, down a back street in Euston with only the sign of the Circle as a guide, check out the floating spiral stairs that run through the building – apparently very popular with staircase enthusiasts. There is barely an empty space on any of the walls; the Magic Circle's members have been collecting tools of the trade since its foundation in 1905 as an organisation to promote the art of magic and protect its secrets. The magicians take their motto, *Indocilis Privata Loqui* (not apt to disclose secrets) seriously.

There are hundreds of vintage posters, but the real glory is the collection of magic props and memorabilia. The Devant Room, named after the first president of the Circle, contains TV legend Tommy Cooper's famous fez. John Nevil Maskelyne, the second president, was a hugely successful magician and also found time to invent the pay toilet lock, source of the expression 'to spend a penny'. Naturally, one of these locks is on display. You can also admire the original working model of Robert Harbin's Zig Zag Girl illusion, which 'chops' a lady into three parts – supposedly the most stolen trick ever.

The museum proper is in the basement and is stuffed with goodies. These include the original Marauder's Map from the 'Harry Potter' films, designed by Magic Circle members; a magical money printer; the shoes Dynamo wore to walk across the Thames (without a bridge); and an original Sooty puppet. The robes of the unfortunate Chung Ling Soo are also on display – this was the stage name of William Robinson, who died onstage at the Wood Green Empire in 1918 after his famous bullet catch trick went wrong.

If you want to duck buying a ticket, you could try joining the Magic Circle. It's not easy, but you do get access to its top-secret inner sanctum and vast library of over 20,000 books on magic. Prince Charles is a member – the props from the cup and ball trick he performed at his audition are on display in the museum – but apparently he doesn't get down there as much as he should.

05.

Gibbs Building, Wellcome Trust, 215 Euston Road, NW1 2BE
Euston Square tube, Euston tube/rail

BLEIGIESSEN

A fortune-telling sculpture

When the Wellcome Trust, the UK's largest medical research charity, redesigned its headquarters on Euston Road, several art works were commissioned to embellish its new premises. The Trust chose Thomas Heatherwick to design the centrepiece: an installation for the ten-storey atrium of the Gibbs Building. The designer faced a serious challenge: while the sculpture had to fill the 30-metre vertical space, its components also had to fit through a regular-sized door. Heatherwick resolved to design something that could fit through a letterbox instead.

Inspired by the pool of water at the bottom of the atrium, Heatherwick based his design on flowing liquid. By pouring molten metal into cold water, he created over 400 prototypes before a five-centimetre shape was selected as the outline for the sculpture. This form was laser-scanned and replicated using 150,000 glass spheres, produced in a Polish spectacle lens factory. Reflective film was sandwiched inside the beads to create a rainbow effect. All the spheres were numbered and assembled on site – a painstaking process, which involved threading the beads onto almost one million metres of steel wire, rolled onto a giant drum then stretched between frames. A team of 18 people worked for five months, day and night, to complete the sculpture, which weighs in at 14 tons. The result is like a glowing cloud of particles suspended in mid-air. Shapes fade in and out of focus depending on how the light strikes.

Heatherwick's German grandmother christened the work Bleigiessen, or 'lead guessing'. This New Year's Eve ritual is still practiced in Eastern Europe: molten lead is poured into cold water, and the resulting shapes are interpreted to predict a person's fortune for the coming year.

The best way to see this monumental work is to take the monthly guided tour. Visitors are whisked to the top of the building in a glass lift. Alternatively, you can get a reasonably good view of the sculpture from Gower Street. It looks best at night when the empty building is illuminated and the baubles shimmer behind the glass walls.

FAKE TREES

The Wellcome Trust contains another secret: half the ficus trees in the soaring atrium are fake. The original trees planted here did not thrive, so their trunks and principal branches were kiln dried and covered with silk leaves.

06.

South Cloisters, University College London, 27–28 Gordon Square, WC1H 0AH
Euston Square, Warren Street or Goodge Street tube

THE AUTO-ICON OF JEREMY BENTHAM

Mummified philosopher

Sitting serenely in a wooden cabinet on a landing of University College London (UCL) is the preserved skeleton of Jeremy Bentham (1748–1832), a radical philosopher and reformer. As stipulated in his will, Bentham has been seated here in the same thoughtful pose, 'wearing his usual clothes and sitting on his favourite chair', since 1850.

Bentham called this perverse monument to himself an Auto-Icon ('man in his own image'), whereby a man's actual corpse replaced the traditional memorial statue. In fact, the body beneath his fine clothes is made of nothing but straw. At a time when only the corpses of hanged criminals were available for medical research, Bentham left his organs 'to illustrate a series of lectures, to which scientific and literary men are to be invited', and then be dissected by students of anatomy. The only part of his body that Bentham did not bequeath to science was his head, which was to be preserved by a Maori practice of desiccation and placed on his Auto-Icon. For ten years before his death, Bentham allegedly carried the glass eyes that were to adorn it in his pocket. Unfortunately, the mummified head deteriorated rapidly, so it was replaced with a less grotesque wax likeness.

For several years, the real head lay between Bentham's legs. However, in 1975, a group of students from King's College 'kidnapped' the head and demanded a ransom of £100 to be paid to the homeless charity Shelter. UCL negotiated the ransom down to £10 and the head was returned to its rightful owner. The head has since been safely stowed in the college vaults; permission to view it is granted 'only in exceptional circumstances'.

Although Bentham was almost 80 when UCL was founded in 1826, as the first English university to welcome all students, regardless of race, creed or political belief, it embodied Bentham's conviction that education should be available to all. Marx may have called him 'genius by way of bourgeois stupidity', but Bentham was a visionary who also believed in universal suffrage, the legalisation of homosexuality, and utilitarianism, a doctrine that aims to promote the greatest happiness of the greatest number.

According to one apocryphal tale, the Auto-Icon attends meetings of the College Council. Its presence is recorded in the minutes with the words 'Jeremy Bentham – present but not voting'. In 2013, the Auto-Icon was indeed wheeled into the last council meeting attended by the provost, Sir Malcom Grant, before he retired.

Visitors' reactions to the mummified philosopher are captured by a webcam mounted above his head. The 'Panopticam' – a tongue-in-cheek reference to Bentham's sinister Panopticon, a circular prison that allowed for the constant surveillance of all inmates – takes a photo every five seconds. An ironic commentary on the desire for self-preservation, or a post-modern critique of the surveillance state?

© Karmakolle

07.

The Petrie Museum, University College London, Malet Place, WC1E 6BT
Euston Square, Goodge Street or Warren Street tube, Euston tube/rail

MIN'S PENIS

Saucy antiquities

Beneath the scholarly air that hangs over this collection of Egyptian and Sudanese antiquities lurk some very saucy artefacts. Set up in 1892 as a teaching resource for University College's Egyptian Archaeology and Philology department, the Petrie Museum is named after the department's first professor, William Flanders Petrie. A serial excavator, Petrie himself unearthed many of the 80,000 objects, dating from pre-history through Pharaonic, Roman, and Coptic Egypt, up to the Islamic period.

Perhaps the most striking exhibit is the marble bas relief of the Egyptian god Min. Invariably portrayed with a huge, erect penis, Min was the god of fertility and sexuality. At the beginning of the harvest, his image was taken out into the fields, where naked men would climb a huge pole in his honour. Apparently, Min used long-leaf lettuce to stimulate his sex drive. However, the results may have been negligible: lettuce was considered an aphrodisiac by the ancient Egyptians because it was tall, straight and secreted milky juices when squeezed.

Costume plays a key part in the collection – look for the world's oldest dress, worn by a dancer around 2500 BCE. Besides extraordinary hieroglyphs and papyri, the plethora of everyday objects includes a 3000-year-old rat trap. There are also strangely affecting Roman funerary masks; since most Egyptian art is nearly abstract, these portraits breathe life into a culture that often feels impassive or monumental.

Although it houses one of the most important Egyptology collections in the world, the Petrie does not punch at the same weight as the Egyptian collection of the British Museum. However, this is to its advantage. The Petrie feels less dependent on plunder than the British Museum, and the collection is more thoughtfully assembled. Access to the Petrie is also easier. The Egyptian funerary rooms at the British Museum, where the most deliciously gruesome stuff is displayed, are usually packed with coach parties; even the vigorous use of knee and elbow is no guarantee of a clear view.

08.

Rockefeller Building, University College London, 21 University Street, WC1E 6DE
Euston Square, Goodge Street or Warren Street tube, Euston tube/rail

THE GRANT MUSEUM OF ZOOLOGY

Dodo bones and jellied eels

One of the oldest – and oddest – natural history museums in Britain, this peculiar collection is buried in the labyrinthine campus of University College London. Navigate a course through the parked bicycles and security gates, and you find yourself in a bizarre shrine to animal anatomy.

The cluttered gallery is like a cross between the Victorian attic of a compulsive collector and the studio of Damien Hirst. Musty cases are stuffed full of monkey skeletons, pickled toads, jars of worms, and giant elephant skulls.

The collection contains around 62,000 specimens, covering the whole animal kingdom. Some of the exhibits are truly terrifying, such as the curling skeleton of a 250-kilo anaconda, or the bisected head of a wallaby preserved in formaldehyde. Others, like the elephant heart or the hellbender – a bloated amphibian with sagging flesh – are simply gruesome.

There are obscure species, like the three-toothed puffer fish, and extinct ones, like the quagga, a type of zebra. There is even a box of dodo bones. A cast of the oldest known bird, the archaeopteryx, provides evidence that birds evolved from dinosaurs. One of the weirdest exhibits is a glass jar stuffed with 18 preserved moles, which even has its own Twitter account (https://twitter.com/GlassJarofMoles).

The museum was founded in 1827 by Robert Grant, a pioneer of the theory of evolution and the first Professor of Zoology and Comparative Anatomy in England. When Grant set up his department at the newly founded University of London (later University College London), he realised that he had no teaching materials. So he set about amassing these specimens, which are still used by biology students, schools, and artists. Although Grant was paid a pittance, he taught at UCL from 1828 until his death in 1874.

Robert Edmond Grant was a Scottish zoologist and radical. While teaching at Edinburgh University in 1826, he met the young Charles Darwin, who was a squeamish and reluctant student of medicine at the time. Grant befriended Darwin and became his mentor, until the two fell out some years later. By a strange twist of fate, Darwin lived in a house on this site, at 12 Upper Gower Street, between 1839 and 1842.

© Grant Museum of Zoology at UCL

© JRennocks

09.

Brunei Gallery, School of Oriental and African Studies
10 Thornhaugh Street, WC1H 0XG
Russell Square tube

JAPANESE ROOF GARDEN

Forgive and forget

Completed in 1937, Senate House – the University of London's Art Deco HQ – was the centrepiece of a grand new campus that would, in the words of Vice-Chancellor William Beveridge, be 'an academic island in swirling tides of traffic, a world of learning in a world of affairs'. By 1939, Europe was at war and the students and professors had been replaced by spies and spin doctors employed at the Ministry of Information – the government's censorship and propaganda machine, which inspired the Ministry of Truth in George Orwell's 'Nineteen Eighty-Four'.

If you want to spy on the university administrators and librarians who work in Senate House, there's a secret garden with a great vantage point over the angular 19-storey tower. Hidden on the roof of the School of Oriental and African Studies' Brunei Gallery – a cool, calm space devoted to art from Asia, Africa and the Middle East – is a formal Japanese garden. There's not much greenery: apart from a dreamy row of benches shaded by wisteria (heavenly in spring) and a few symmetrically planted squares of lemon thyme, it's mostly artfully placed pebbles, immaculately raked gravel and slabs of grey rock. The effect, though austere, is deeply soothing.

Look out for the granite water feature engraved with the Japanese symbol for forgiveness. There's a raised 'stage' at one end for occasional concerts, performances, and tea and flower ceremonies.

The Brunei Gallery always had a roof garden; the original one featured a series of pools, which sprang a leak and had to be drained. So it was eventually replaced with this low-maintenance design.

Most of the time, especially on Saturdays, the garden is deserted. So you can just sit quietly and let the swirl of the surrounding city drift away...

ISMAILI CENTRE ROOF GARDEN

London's most spectacular roof garden is on top of the Ismaili Centre, a cubist monolith that seems to shun visitors. Screened from the traffic roaring down Cromwell Road, this elegant garden is as reclusive as the Ismailis' spiritual and political leader, the Aga Khan. The geometric design alludes to the Qu'ranic garden of paradise, with a central fountain connected to four granite pools that symbolise the celestial rivers flowing with water, honey, milk and wine. Sadly, it's only open on Open Garden Squares Weekend (londongardenstrust.org).

© Brunei Gallery, SOAS University of London

10.

Colonnade Bloomsbury, WC1N 1JD
Russell Square tube

THE HORSE HOSPITAL

Salon of the avant garde

Buried away down a cobbled mews off tourist-trodden Russell Square, the Horse Hospital really was a sanctuary for sick horses back in its Victorian heyday. These days, it's a haven for avant-garde artists and disciples of all things underground. From the blood red hall, a steep ramp with wooden slats originally intended to stop the horses slipping (beware – it's lethal in heels) leads down to a slightly spooky and faintly musty salon with a few battered seats. Mismatched cobblestones echo underfoot. Other original features, including tethering rings, cast iron pillars, and barred windows, have a whiff of S&M about them.

This is the self-styled Chamber of Pop Culture, where an audience of eccentrics enjoy the most eclectic line-up of art events in London, from cult films to performance poets, clairvoyant workshops and queer porn. Anything goes – as long as it's defiantly anti-establishment. The small bar at the back is one of those rare places in London where you can easily slip into conversation with strangers. This sense of community, along with the spirit of experimentation, is like a throwback to the Arts Labs of the '60s.

Often dubbed 'an alternative ICA', the Horse Hospital was founded in 1993 by stylist and costume designer Richard Burton, one of the pioneers of punk fashion along with Vivienne Westwood and Malcolm McLaren, whose original boutique, World's End, was designed by Burton. The Horse Hospital opened with a splash 13 years later with the first retrospective of Westwood's punk designs. It's run on a shoestring by a staff of two: Burton and programmer Tai Shani. Long may they continue to celebrate culture that champions 'the outsider, the unfashionable and the other'.

CONTEMPORARY WARDROBE COLLECTION

The upper floor of the Horse Hospital is home to the Contemporary Wardrobe Collection, set up by Burton in 1978 to supply vintage clothes and accessories to the film, TV and fashion industries. His collection now exceeds 15,000 garments dating back to 1945. There's a rare selection by seminal British designers from the 1960s, such as Ossie Clark, Biba, and Seditionaries. As well as providing costumes for films like *Quadrophenia* and *Sid & Nancy*, pieces have been modelled by over 400 pop stars, from the late, great David Bowie to Kanye West. Visits are by appointment only. Twice a year, items are sold off to raise funds for The Horse Hospital.
Check contemporarywardrobe.com for details.

11.

40 Brunswick Square, WC1N 1AZ
Russell Square tube, King's Cross or Euston tube /rail

THE FOUNDLING MUSEUM

Children lost and found

There is a lingering idea among tourists that London is a place of Victorian propriety, full of well-mannered, uptight ladies and gentlemen. Apart from a very brief 19th-century flirtation with moral rectitude, the character of the city has always been base; drunkenness for its own sake is still very much a London pastime, as is fighting. This wildness and cruelty was at its apogee in the 18th century, when a man could be hanged for stealing spoons.

One by-product of a society like this was hordes of unwanted children. Up to a thousand babies a year were abandoned in the streets of London in the early 18th century. Fortunately, in 1739, after 17 years of tireless fundraising, the philanthropist Thomas Coram founded a 'Hospital for the Maintenance and Education of Exposed and Deserted Children', which cared for more than 27,000 children at a site on Lamb's Conduit Fields, before relocating to the countryside in 1953. The remarkable Foundling Museum tells the story of those children.

Thanks to William Hogarth, one of the original governors of the hospital, the museum also houses an impressive art collection, displayed in interiors restored to their original 18th-century condition. Hogarth's own art is often hard-bitten and deeply cynical – his famous etching of Gin Lane is full of disgust at how the people who abandoned these children lived. But there must have been a well of compassion in him: Hogarth persuaded leading artists like Gainsborough and Reynolds to donate works to the hospital, and in doing so created the country's first public exhibition space. This eventually led to the formation of the Royal Academy of Arts in 1768. In keeping with its founding principles, most of The Foundling Museum's workshops and concerts are aimed at children.

The peaceful café is run by The People's Supermarket, a not-for-profit grocery store on Lamb's Conduit Street, run by local volunteers.

HANDEL & HENDRIX

The German composer George Friedrich Handel was also a one-time governor of the hospital, which explains why the museum holds a collection of Handel material. Annual performances of his Messiah provided a source of revenue for the hospital. Today, you can catch live music by Handel and his contemporaries every Thursday at Handel & Hendrix (handelhendrix.org), the composer's former home at 25 Brook Street, Mayfair. Rock star Jimi Hendrix lived next door at 23 Brook Street in 1968-9. Now open to the public, Hendrix's third-floor flat has a few psychedelic flourishes, but presents a surprisingly domesticated picture.

12.

60 Great Queen Street, Holborn, WC2B 5AZ
Holborn or Covent Garden tube

FREEMASONS' HALL

Yes, the Freemasons' Hall is open to the public

Time was when everyone thought there was nothing more secretive than a Freemason. But since the 1980s, the holiest of holies, the Freemasons' Hall near Covent Garden, has been open to the public, with a dedicated museum, an exhibition space in its library, and free hour-long tours of the building including the Grand Temple.

Opened in 1933 when freemasonry was flourishing, the hall is an art deco beast of a building that dominates the street. It is often used as a film location and has doubled as Saddam Hussein's palace. There is something melancholic about the place; membership numbers are in decline, which undoubtedly lies behind the decision to modernise and open up. The museum does a good job of explaining the history of freemasonry in the UK, and how the medieval stonemasons' guilds, with their secret words and symbols, were adapted to become the guiding model for the organisation.

Highlights include a display of Masonic regalia, including ornate aprons and gauntlet cuffs, items belonging to famous Freemasons including King Edward VII and Winston Churchill, and best of all, the colossal Grand Master's Throne. Built in 1791, its first occupant was the Prince Regent, later George IV. George was notoriously fat – in his later years, he had to sleep sitting up in order to breathe – and the chair looks as if it was designed with his elephantine backside in mind.

The glory of the hall, however, is the Grand Temple. Enter it through bronze doors that each weigh over a tonne, and gaze up at its 18-metre mosaic ceiling. The grand days of the brotherhood may be behind them, but they're still well housed.

HE SHALL BUILD ME AN HOUSE
AND I WILL STABLISH HIS
ESTABLISHED FOR EVERMORE
THRONE FOR EVER

13.

British Museum, Great Russell Street, WC1B 3DG
Russell Square or Tottenham Court Road tube

THE MUMMY OF KATEBET

Black magic in Ancient Egypt

In room 63 on the Upper Level of the British Museum, the mummy of a nearly toothless elderly woman is said to be that of Katebet. Her embalmers did not extract her brain during the mummification process, which is extremely unusual. Katebet has been identified as a woman who lived in Thebes, Egypt, around 1300–1280 BCE. She was a priestess–princess of the god Amon, singing hymns to his praise in his temple.

Mysteries surround the sarcophagus and all the decorations on the mummy. The position of the hands and the shape of the wig are those associated with mummies of men, not women. Likewise, some of the objects placed on the mummy were usually intended for a man. At one time, it was thought that the mummy was that of her husband, Quenna, with whom Katebet would have been entombed. But no trace of his mummy has ever been found, and in fact, his very existence is seriously doubted. The gilded face is framed by a wig from which white ear studs peek out. The hands, crossed over the chest, are adorned with royal rings suggesting magical phallic signs. A small, dark scarab sits on her stomach. It is surmounted by a human face with outspread wings representing the soul (*Ka* in Egyptian). Two figures, a man and a woman, flank the scarab. They are probably priests of Amon, put there to provide magical protection. A mummy-shaped figurine is embossed lower down, at knee level. This *shabti* indicates that Katebet was mummified according to the dictates of the official religion of Thebes at the time. According to esoteric theosophical doctrine, however, this mummy is actually that of Kali-Beth (the 'Black Princess'), sister of Thutmose II, fourth pharaoh of the 18th Dynasty. She was descended from an ancient sorcerer-king named Baal-Iman (the 'Crow King') who, it is said, finally succumbed to the evil in the black magic he practised.

Due to Kali-Beth's beauty, vivacity and unsavoury ancestry, the sorcerers of Thebes who were her contemporaries hatched a plot to kidnap her and mummify her alive. They claimed to know spells that could trap her soul within her embalmed body. This would make her a statue with an immortal, eternally functioning mind. Her Ka, imprisoned by her improperly mummified body, would rear up and become a terrifying monster, driven by an insatiable desire for revenge. Kali-Beth's murderers hoped to make her suffer such torments that powerful vibrations of pain, hatred and

© Gary Todd

rebellion would forever emanate from her soul. Desecrated, the body would become a valuable source of evil energies. The curse of this mummy was so sinister that wherever it dwelt, all sorts of misfortunes would befall the populace. By inspiring such terror, the sorcerers of Thebes ruled every aspect of life in the region. They were the political, economic, military, social and even religious authorities.

Meanwhile, Thutmose III ascended to the throne of Egypt and married Princess Satiah. The couple's great spiritual and human dignity led them to abjure the sorcerers, who supported their rival Hatshepsut. Hatshepsut was the half-sister and wicked stepmother of the young Thutmose. During his childhood, she had governed as a cruel despot.

Shortly before he was crowned king, Thutmose III and Satiah nearly met the same fate as Kali-Beth. Hatshepsut had ordered her royal sorcerers to kidnap the couple, mummify the prince alive and place him in the same sarcophagus as Kali-Beth. The idea was to replace the rotten body of the ancient princess, which was no longer useful. At the last minute, a group of warriors and priests loyal to Thutmose III burst into the sorcerers' lair and killed them. They burnt down the temple and threw old Hatshepsut into jail. It is said that she was subjected to the same torture as Kali-Beth but that her mortal remains were thrown onto the funeral pyre in order to purify the perverted shrine.

The symbols on the sarcophagus do clearly suggest black magic. The scarab on the stomach is an avatar of Khepra, the goddess of cosmic harmony, peace and justice. However, the hand signals made by the mummy are known to counteract and disrupt Khepra's powers.

The position of the fingers on the right hand refers to the phallic symbol of Saturn and the attachment to lust and material instincts. The scarab symbolises the rebirth of the soul. Its position indicates that the soul of Kali-Beth is artificially trapped inside her body. With her left hand, the princess is making the sign of the bull's horns. A symbol of virility, the horns also signify infidelity when made by the left hand.

14.

Fitzroy Place, 2 Pearson Square, W1T 3BF
Goodge Street tube

FITZROVIA CHAPEL

Pocket-sized luxury

Tucked away in the heart of a new residential development north of Soho, Fitzrovia Chapel is a little golden jewel box of a building which is all that remains of the Middlesex Hospital. Opened in the 1740s, the hospital evolved from a 15-bed operation to a leading teaching hospital, with the first dedicated AIDS wards in the UK. It finally closed in 2005 and was consolidated with University College Hospital round the corner on Euston Road. Officially opened by the Bishop of London in 1892, the chapel was designed by John Loughborough Pearson, who was well known as an ecclesiastical architect at the end of the 19th century. Typically, he appears to have worked on a massive scale, designing Bristol and Truro Cathedrals, as well as St Augustine's, Kilburn, an overwrought barn of a church sometimes called the Cathedral of North London and worth a visit.

For the Fitzrovia Chapel, Pearson was forced to work in miniature on a cramped site at the north-western corner of the main hospital building. Limitations of space don't appear to have dampened his enthusiasm for the ornate, however: although the exterior is plain red brick and dressed Portland stone, he seems to have managed to squeeze a whole cathedral's worth of gold and marble into the interior.

This took time – the mosaic ceiling was still being worked on in 1936 for the lying-in-state of Rudyard Kipling – but eventually, Pearson's 'expensive' design was finished, just in time for the Second World War and the Blitz, during which the hospital was bombed. The chapel has been fully restored as part of the conditions of sale of the hospital site to the current developers, and is open to the public one day a week.

GOTHIC REVIVALIST

Pearson was a prominent Gothic Revivalist. This style of architecture, which originated in the UK, sought to recreate medieval Gothic architecture. Pugin's Palace of Westminster is the best-known example in London, but the capital is full of it. Strawberry Hill House in Richmond is the earliest example of the style in the UK – frankly, it's bananas and well worth a trip. Tower Bridge and St Pancras station are good examples of how the Victorians sought to romanticise the most functional of buildings, using the style. Bear in mind that these two were built at around the same time as the Eiffel Tower and the Brooklyn Bridge, both of which still feel modern by comparison.

15.

Broadwick Street, W1F 9QJ
Oxford Circus or Piccadilly Circus tube

JOHN SNOW'S CHOLERA PUMP

Drink beer, not water

Soho has always had its insalubrious side. As Judith Summers writes in 'A History of London's Most Colourful Neighborhood': 'By the middle of the 19th century, Soho had become an unsanitary place of cow-sheds, animal droppings, slaughterhouses, grease-boiling dens and primitive, decaying sewers. And underneath the floorboards of the overcrowded cellars lurked something even worse – a fetid sea of cesspits as old as the houses, and many of which had never been drained. It was only a matter of time before this hidden festering time-bomb exploded. It finally did so in the summer of 1854.'

In September 1854 alone, 500 Soho residents died of cholera. Dr John Snow, an anaesthetist and epidemiologist who lived on Soho Square, concluded that the polluted water pump on Broad Street (as it was called then) had caused the epidemic. Initially, the establishment scoffed at Snow's theory. The Reverend Henry Whitehead, vicar of St Luke's church on nearby Berwick Street, claimed the deceased were the victims of divine intervention. But soon after Snow forcibly removed the handle of the water pump, the outbreak ended.

In his research into the causes of the disease, Dr Snow had to look no further than the Broad Street brewery. One of the perks of employees was an allowance of free beer, so they all abstained from drinking water. None of the 70 workers caught cholera.

For years, a replica water pump stood on the corner of Broadwick and Poland Street. It was removed in 2015 to accommodate the construction of an office block. Westminster Council has pledged to return the pump to its original location, outside the John Snow, a cosy old boozer pub on the corner of Broadwick and Lexington Street. A pink granite kerbstone outside the pub marks the spot where the original pump stood.

Ironically, Snow himself was teetotal. Aged 23, he gave an impassioned speech railing against 'drunkenness in all its hideousness' and 'the physical evils sustained to your health by using intoxicating liquors even in the greatest moderation'. Something to ponder as you settle into the John Snow's snug.

John Snow was already famous for an earlier discovery in 1853: chloroform.

Queen Victoria used this primitive anaesthetic to overcome the agonies of labour during the birth of her son, Prince Leopold. But Snow's medical research did not help his own health; he died of a stroke in 1858, aged 45.

THE SOHO CHOLERA EPIDEMIC
THIS WATER PUMP
WAS UNVEILED BY
COUNCILLOR DAVID WEEKS
ON
20 JULY 1992

16.

5 Leicester Place, WC2H 7BX
Leicester Square tube

THE JEAN COCTEAU MURALS AT NOTRE-DAME DE FRANCE

Cocteau does Soho

The French have been in London for a very long time. The first great influx was that of the Huguenots in 1675, who built fortunes in the textile industry in the East End. Notre-Dame de France is the most recent incarnation of a Catholic church that has been rebuilt several times since it was founded in 1865 to take care of the 'lower-class French' of London. Soho was, until relatively recently, a French enclave; this is one of the ghosts of that time. The original church was designed by Louis Auguste Boileau as a rotunda made entirely out of iron, and not surprisingly was quite a local talking point. This was bombed out in 1940, and the current church was inaugurated in 1955 after two years of construction.

The glory of the church is the artwork within it, above all the murals by legendary French filmmaker, artist, and designer Jean Cocteau, which fill one side chapel. Cocteau came to London to paint the murals in November 1959. Such was his fame that a screen was erected to keep the public and press at bay while he painted the murals in just nine days. Depicting themes from the Crucifixion and the Assumption of Mary, the work is vigorous, sexy and full of life in a manner quite unlike British religious art. Oddities include a black sun, and the fact that the viewer can only see the feet of Christ, as muscular soldiers in tiny skirts play dice for his robe at the base of the Cross. Cocteau included a self-portrait in the mural. Apparently, he was transported while painting it, talking to the figures as he worked.

In 2003, rendering work led to the rediscovery of a mosaic of the nativity, outlined in brilliant enamel by Boris Anrep, a Russian artist best known for his mosaics in Westminster Cathedral and the National Gallery.

Cocteau had deliberately covered up Anrep's work, which infuriated the latter. In 2012, an unknown vandal added his own cryptic signature (T_A*) to one of the paintings, and drew a circle around Cocteau's sun. The restored murals are now displayed behind glass panels.

Unlike so many other churches in London, Notre Dame, which also operates a refugee centre, is very much alive. Other notable features in the church are the tapestry above the altar by Robert De Caunac, depicting Mary as the new Eve, and a vast statue of the Virgin of Mercy by Georges Saupique, who made the sculptures of the Palais du Trocadéro in Paris. Light a candle, as Cocteau did every morning before he set to work, then plunge into the fleshpots of Soho and Leicester Square.

17.

Behind 7 St James's Street, SW1A 1EA
Green Park tube

PICKERING PLACE

Last bastion of the Republic of Texas

Pay close attention when looking for this tiny courtyard tucked away behind swanky St James's Street. If the gate is closed, the only indication you are at Pickering Place is the number 3 on it. The narrow, arched alleyway leading to the courtyard retains its 18th-century timber wainscoting. A relatively unspoilt Georgian cul-de-sac still lit by original gaslights, Pickering Place is named after William Pickering, the founder of a coffee business in the premises now occupied by the famous wine merchants Berry Bros. & Rudd.

Graham Greene, who lived in a flat in Pickering Place, housed his fictional character Colonel Daintry from 'The Human Factor' in a two-roomed flat looking out over the paved courtyard with its sundial. In real life, Pickering Place was the base of the diplomatic office of the independent Republic of Texas, before it joined the United States in 1845.

In the 18th century, Pickering Place was notorious for its gambling dens. Its seclusion also made it a favourite spot for duels, although the limited space suggests that fooling around with any kind of weapon – let alone pistols – would have been instantly fatal. It is claimed that the last duel in England was fought here, although an episode with pistols between two Frenchmen at Windsor in 1852 is the more likely contender. Beau Brummel, a notorious dandy and friend of King George IV, is also said to have fought here. But it is hard to imagine the man who invented the cravat, took five hours to dress, and recommended that boots be polished with champagne, having anything to do with bloodshed. Indeed, Brummel embarked upon a military career as a young man, but promptly resigned his commission when he learned that his regiment was to be sent to Manchester.

18.

Outside the Athenaeum Club, 107 Pall Mall, St James's, SW1Y 5ER
Piccadilly tube

MOUNTING BLOCK

A step fit for a duke

On the pavement outside the Athenaeum private members' club, it is easy to miss a two-levelled granite step about a metre long. A forgotten necessity from the days of horse riding, this was once used by the Duke of Wellington himself as he climbed off and on his noble steed and galloped about the city.

Defeating Napoleon at the Battle of Waterloo in 1815, and serving as Prime Minister not once but twice, has made the Duke of Wellington (aka Arthur Wellesley) an icon of British history. Although his other memorials are far more famous (for example, the Wellington Arch at Hyde Park Corner or the Wellington Monument on Park Lane), his personal horse-step is completely overlooked by the millions of people making their way up and down Pall Mall.

Wellesley was a loyal member of the Athenaeum and, six years after the club was founded in 1824, he (then Prime Minister) suggested they place some stone steps outside the entrance to help the many elderly club members who arrived by horseback to dismount gracefully.

The Duke of Wellington had a war horse called Copenhagen, who he famously rode into the battle at Waterloo. A mixed thoroughbred with Arabian parentage, Copenhagen quickly became Wellesley's favourite horse. But as Copenhagen was mostly used for military service, processions and racing, it is not known whether he ever graced the steps of the Athenaeum.

THE ATHENAEUM CLUB

The Athenaeum has been a prestigious private members' club since its founding almost 200 years ago. It was designed by Decimus Burton in the neoclassical style and has a statue of Athena (the Greek goddess of wisdom and the club's namesake) guarding the entrance. Although the club was designed to be non-partisan, it was still careful to admit only those who it thought would create an atmosphere of 'learning': alongside the Duke of Wellington, it boasts famous alumni such as Charles Darwin, Winston Churchill, Charles Dickens, Arthur Conan Doyle, Joseph Conrad and Thomas Hardy.

19.

Next to 9 Carlton House Terrace, SW1Y 5AG
Piccadilly Circus or Charing Cross tube

GIRO'S GRAVE

Epitaph to an ambassador's pooch

Between St James's Park and Piccadilly Circus, Waterloo Place was designed by the 19th-century architect John Nash as an overblown testament to the splendour of the British Empire. Countless statues of heroic commanders and louche aristocrats vie to outdo each other in size and stature. Buried among these grand memorials, a tiny tombstone lies at the foot of an enormous tree between the Duke of York Steps and an underground garage. Shielded by what appears to be a miniature kennel, the German epitaph on the gravestone reads: '*Giro, ein treuer Begleiter! London, im Februar 1934, Hoesch*'. This 'true companion', Giro, was the beloved dog of the German Ambassador, Leopold von Hoesch, who served in London from 1932 to 1936. Now fenced off by railings, his grave lies on a patch of land that was once the garden of the ambassador's residence at 9 Carlton House Terrace.

The hapless Giro met his maker after colliding with an electricity cable while scampering about in what is now the Institute of Contemporary Arts. Apocryphal reports suggest that Giro received a full Nazi burial, though this seems highly unlikely since Hoesch was openly opposed to the rise of the Third Reich. The strain proved too much for Hoesch, who died of a stroke in 1936. The ambassador was granted a state funeral. But the Nazis had the last laugh: his coffin was swaddled in a giant swastika and embassy staff gave the Nazi salute as the funeral cortège marched by.

THE MARBLE STAIRCASE OF MUSSOLINI

After Hoesch's replacement – and Hitler's close associate – Joachim von Ribbentrop moved into Carlton House Terrace, the Führer's favourite architect, Albert Speer, was dispatched to London to give the embassy a flashy revamp. The British government did not deport Hitler's diplomats until 1939, when the building was taken over by the Foreign Office and stripped of its Nazi trappings – although a staircase of Italian marble, donated by Mussolini, is apparently still intact.

"GIRO"

20.

Trafalgar Square, WC2N 5DP
Charing Cross or Leicester Square tube

BRITAIN'S SMALLEST POLICE STATION

A peeping pillar

On the south-east corner of Trafalgar Square, surely London's biggest tourist trap, is Britain's smallest police station. The hordes of tourists posing before Nelson's Column and clambering on Sir Edwin Landseer's bronze lions are oblivious to this one-man sentry box fashioned from a hollowed-out granite lamp post. Allegedly, the secret police box was installed by Scotland Yard in 1926 so that the cops could keep an eye on the demonstrators and agitators who routinely gathered in Trafalgar Square (still London's most popular protest site). With its narrow slits for windows and claustrophobic proportions, this human CCTV camera must have been even more unpleasant during a riot. It was equipped with a telephone with a direct line to Canon Row Police Station in case things got out of hand.

Originally installed in 1826, the ornamental light on the top is probably not from Nelson's HMS Victory, as some guides would have you believe.

However, it did flash whenever the police officer trapped inside picked up the telephone, alerting any fellow officers in the vicinity to come to his rescue.

Today, the lookout post is used to store street cleaning equipment. The only clue that it has links to the police is a faded list of by-laws hanging outside.

For the record, offences in Trafalgar Square include feeding birds, camping, parking a caravan, public speaking, playing music, washing or drying clothes, exercising, bathing, boating or canoeing in the fountains, flying a kite, or using any 'foot-propelled device' – unless you have written permission from the Mayor.

21.

42 Craven Street, WC2N 5NG
Charing Cross or Embankment tube

THE BRITISH OPTICAL ASSOCIATION MUSEUM

Eyeballs galore

In the basement of a fine Georgian terrace a stone's throw from Trafalgar Square, this obscure but delightful museum contains thousands of eye-catching objects relating to the history of optometry. Founded in 1901, the collection includes over 3,000 pairs of eyeglasses. There are pince-nez, lorgnettes, magnifiers, quizzing glasses, goggles and monocles, opera glasses with secret snuff compartments, 'jealousy glasses' with lenses concealed in the sides, rose-tinted sunglasses, wig spectacles that slid into your hairpiece, and all manner of fancy spectacle receptacles.

There are celebrity specs, including Dr Johnson, Ronnie Corbett and Dr Crippen, and Leonardo de Caprio's contact lenses. Some models – like the windscreen wiper glasses with battery attached and a spring-loaded contraption to catapult contact lenses into the eyeball – did not take off.

Curator Neil Handley gives every visitor a personal guided tour, pointing out rare items such as an ancient Egyptian amulet of the eye of Horus, ensuring the dead could see in the afterlife, and a 16th-century statue of Saint Odilia, bearing two eyeballs on a bible. The optometric instruments are historical eye-openers, such as a Victorian self-testing machine with a religious text, designed to improve users' morals as well as their vision. Visitors can test their eyesight in a 1930s optician's chair with a built-in refraction unit, try on different frames, or explore foreign cities through an early View-Master. A drawer full of artificial, diseased, deformed and injured eyes, dating from 1880, is definitely not for the squeamish.

For a fee, you can also view the portraits of bespectacled sitters and optically-themed prints and satirical drawings in the meeting rooms on the first floor.

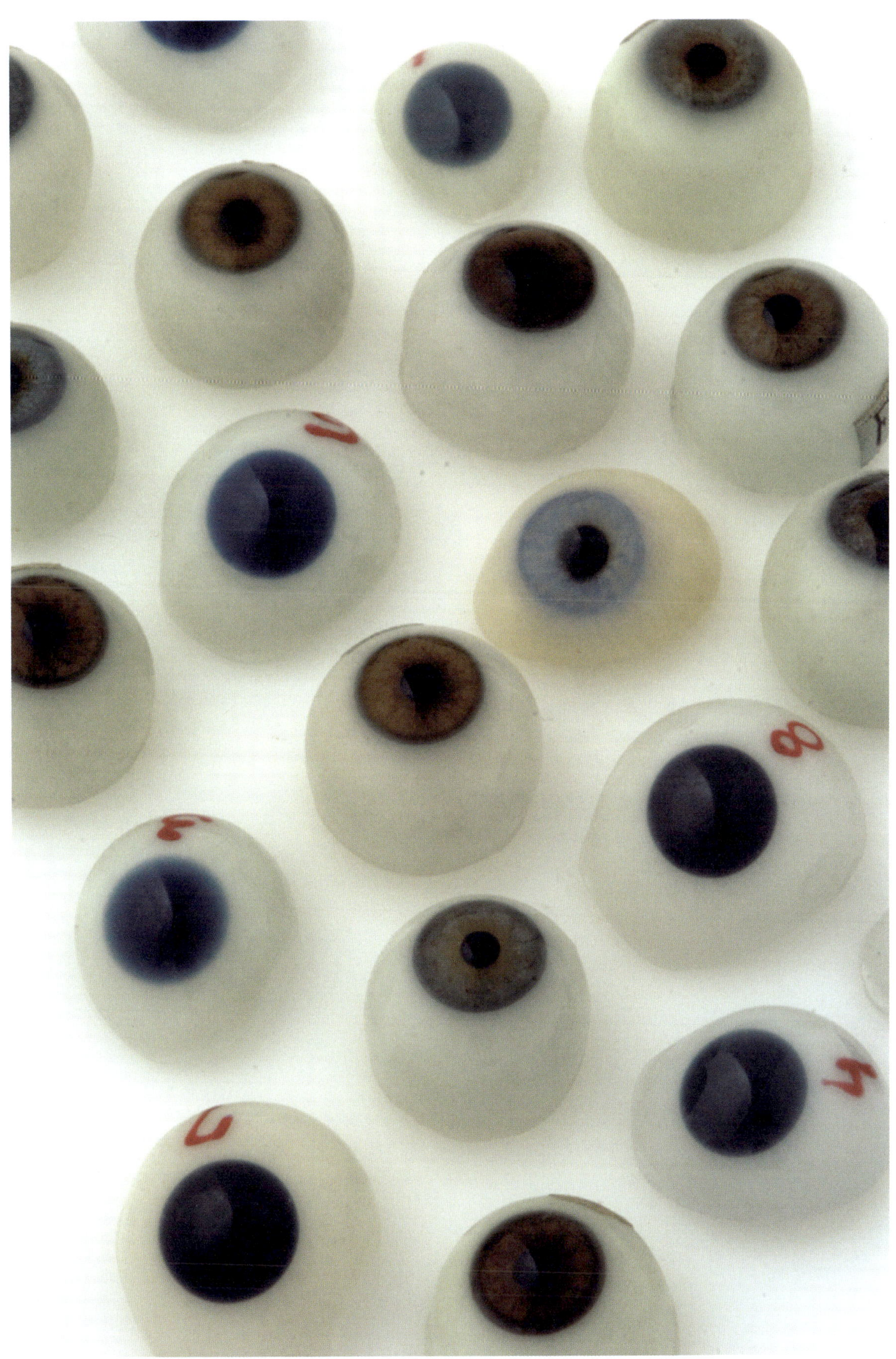

22.

The Sherlock Holmes, 10 Northumberland Street, WC2N 5DB
Charing Cross or Embankment tube

SHERLOCK HOLMES ROOM

Dining next to the detectives

221b Baker Street is by far the best-known fictional address in London. However, as conceived by Arthur Conan Doyle, the rooms where Sherlock Holmes and Dr John Watson lived never actually existed – at the time the stories were written, house numbers on the street only went as high as 85 before Baker Street became York Place. In the 1930s, Baker Street was extended. The Abbey National Building Society moved into 219–229 Baker Street, and a full-time secretary was employed to answer mail addressed to the great detective.

In 1951, as part of the Festival of Britain, the building society staged an exhibition at its offices, re-creating the sitting room of 221b according to the plans of theatre designer Michael Weight. The exhibition was so successful that it was relocated to New York in 1952. In 1957, it was moved again: brewing giants Whitbread refurbished a small hotel they owned called the Northumberland Arms, and reopened it as The Sherlock Holmes.

The pub is full of Holmesiana, but the *pièce de résistance* is the Sherlock Holmes Room, reconstructed in a closed-off corner of the restaurant on the first floor. It's a little bit odd – you stare through the glass while oblivious diners eat away – but the attention to detail is worth it. There are clues from stories including 'The Red-Headed League' and 'The Adventure of the Dancing Men'.

As well as vials of borax, and Holmes's violin and famous deerstalker, there's a wax dummy of the detective with a bullet wound in his forehead, a reference to 'The Adventure of the Empty House'.

Of course, the real Holmes survived 'to devote his life to examining those interesting little problems which the complex life of London so plentifully presents'.

THE FESTIVAL OF BRITAIN

This national exhibition was held in 1951 to engender a sense of recovery and hope after the Second World War. London was the centre of the festival, which must have been a tricky proposition – rationing was in place until 1954 and large parts of the city were still bombsites. Most of the exhibition was temporary. The South Bank Exhibition was demolished (with the exception of the Royal Festival Hall, still going strong). The Festival Pleasure Gardens in Battersea Park have also survived – well worth a visit for their 1950s feel.

The
RED-HEADED
LEAGUE IS
DISSOLVED

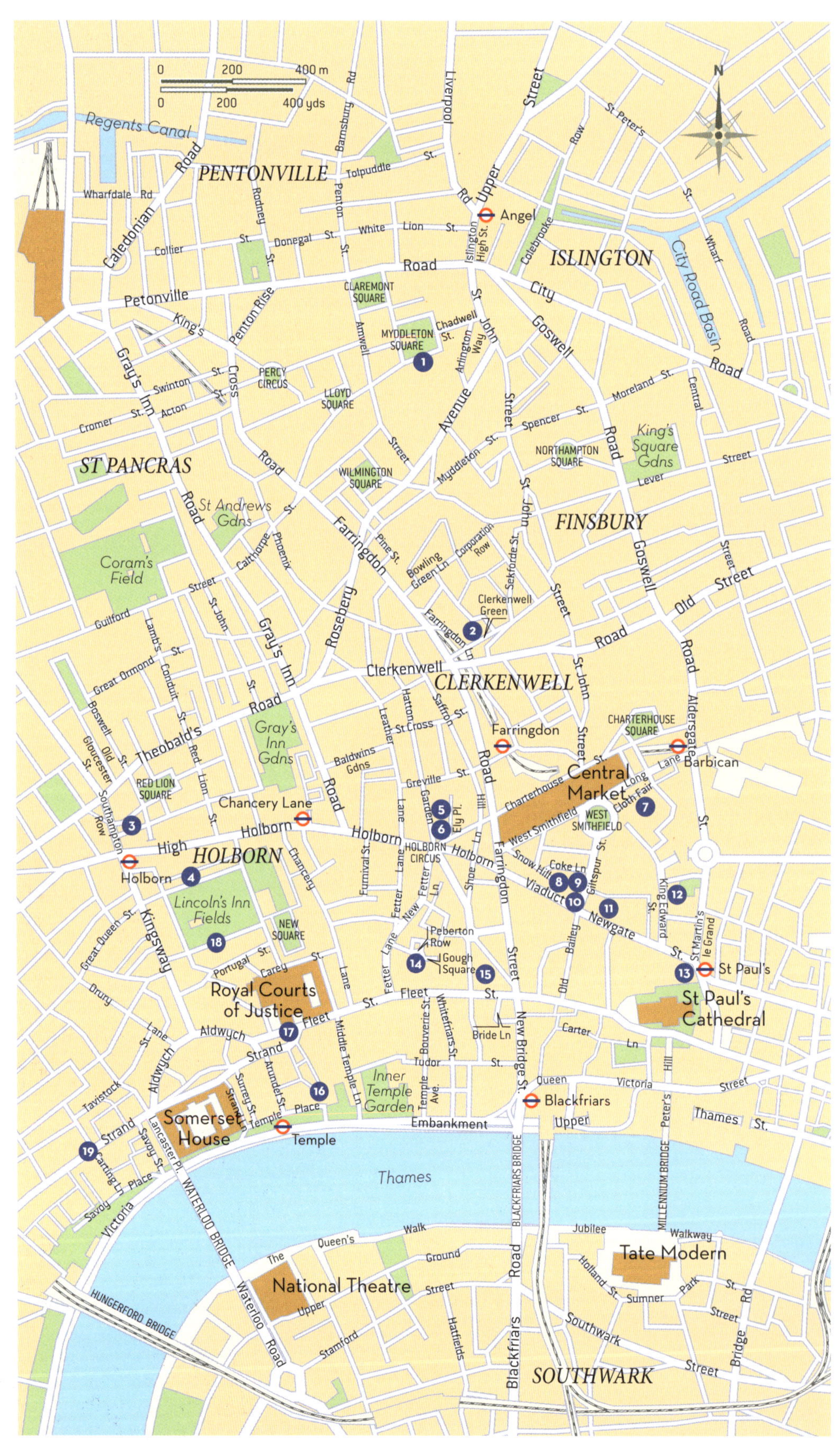
PENTONVILLE
ISLINGTON
ST PANCRAS
FINSBURY
CLERKENWELL
HOLBORN
SOUTHWARK
Angel
Farringdon
Barbican
Chancery Lane
Holborn
St Paul's
Blackfriars
Temple
Central Market
Royal Courts of Justice
St Paul's Cathedral
Somerset House
National Theatre
Tate Modern
Thames
Coram's Field
Lincoln's Inn Fields
Gray's Inn Gdns
Inner Temple Garden
King's Square Gdns
St Andrews Gdns
Regents Canal
City Road Basin
BLACKFRIARS BRIDGE
MILLENNIUM BRIDGE
WATERLOO BRIDGE
HUNGERFORD BRIDGE

ANGEL TO TEMPLE

01.

Myddelton Square, EC1R 1YE
Angel tube

MYDDELTON PASSAGE CARVINGS

The inscriptions of bored Victorian police officers

At the bottom of Myddelton Square, a beautiful open space lined with Georgian-style terraces, is a scruffy wall marked with numbers and letters. For a long time, these mysterious carvings were thought to be the work of rebellious prisoners during the Napoleonic wars: it was assumed that they had etched their prisoner numbers into the bricks. Over the centuries, more and more vandals added their identification numbers to the wall. This theory was disproved by the sharp mind of Peter Guillery, an English Heritage researcher who was creating a mass survey of historic London: he presented a brand-new theory about the origins of the carvings. In 2006 Guillery reported that the marks had been made by on-duty Victorian policemen who were bored, possibly drunk and looking for amusement. The idea was a suggestion by an old retired police officer and Guillery's research, aided by Margaret Bird from the Metropolitan Police Service historical archives, proved this explanation correct. If you look closely at the carvings, you'll see that most of them have a 'G' in the sequence. After some sleuthing, it was decided that this stood for the 'G division' of the Metropolitan Police who operated out of Kings Cross in the 19th century. The numbers before the division letter were the policemen's 'collar' number – the unique series of identification numbers given to every recruit at the start of their career. Usually, this number was also displayed on their uniform, so if the carvings really were personalised graffiti by officers of the law, then it would have been very easy to identify the individuals who carried out this petty crime! Incredibly, some of these police officers have now been identified through archival research – for example, Frederick Albert Moore of G Division ('365 Plymouth' on the wall).

Lucky for them that it took a few hundred years to figure out exactly what the sequences were …

02.

37a Clerkenwell Green, EC1R 0DU
Farringdon tube

MARX MEMORIAL LIBRARY

Lenin's London office

The bright red door is the only clue to what lies inside this Georgian townhouse that sits inconspicuously beside the snazzy jewellery and architecture studios of Clerkenwell Green. A brass plaque by the doorbell proclaims that this is the Marx Memorial Library, home to over 150,000 volumes of leftist literature.

From the Peasants' Revolt in 1381 to the Poll Tax demonstrations of the 1980s, this quaint corner of London has long been a breeding ground for rebels, rioters, and political refugees. Among them was Vladimir Ilyich Ulyanov who in 1902-3 shared space in this building with Harry Quelch, editor of the left-wing Twentieth Century Press. Lenin's poky office is intact, with its blue cupboards, leather-bound socialist tracts, a Braille edition of the Communist Manifesto, and countless busts of the man himself donated by admirers. This is where Lenin edited issues 22-38 of his Russian newspaper Iskra (The Spark), printed on extra thin paper so it was easier to smuggle into Tsarist Russia.

Built in 1737 as a charitable school for Welsh boys, the building acquired its first radical residents when the London Patriotic Society arrived in 1872. The Marx Memorial Library and Workers' School was established 1933, on the 50th anniversary of Marx's death, as an angry response to the public burning of books in Nazi Germany. In 1935, Viscount Jack Hastings, an aristocratic Communist and pupil of the Mexican radical artist Diego Riviera, painted a giant mural grandly titled 'Worker of the Future Clearing Away the Chaos of Capitalism'; the figures of Marx, Engels, and Lenin loom larger than life behind the reception desk. Downstairs, the archive of the International Brigade has pride of place in a meeting room decked with revolutionary posters. The library's red shelves and blue linoleum floors are scuffed, old-fashioned, slightly down at heel – exactly as they should be. In keeping with its socialist principles, membership costs just £25 a year (£15 for concessions).

In 1986, some 14th-century tunnels were discovered in the basement, which can be viewed on Open House weekend.

MARX IN LONDON

Karl Marx wrote much of 'Das Kapital' seated in Chair G7 at the British Museum Reading Room. In 1850-55, Marx lived in a squalid apartment above what is now the Quo Vadis restaurant in Soho. But the restaurant's original owner, Peppino Leoni, was loath to have a blue plaque commemorating a communist outside his fancy establishment at 28 Dean Street.

MARX MEMORIAL LIBRARY
AND WORKERS' SCHOOL
WORKERS OF ALL
LANDS UNITE

03.

Southampton Row, WC2
Holborn Tube

KINGSWAY TRAM SUBWAY

Tracks from the past

If you are brave enough to dodge the traffic roaring down Kingsway, in the middle of Southampton Row, just beyond Holborn tube station, is a ramp leading to a disused tunnel. This is one of the last vestiges of London's tram network, which criss-crossed the city until the early 1950s.

The gates to the tunnel are now permanently locked, but if you peek through the railings you can see the old tram tracks running along the cobblestones. Between the tracks, you can just make out the underground electricity cable that powered the trams along this route from Angel to Aldwych. It took just ten minutes to make the journey from Islington to Waterloo Bridge – an enviable record by today's standards. Built in 1906, the two-way tunnel originally passed though a subterranean station at Holborn, and then down the length of Kingsway to another tram stop at Aldwych, before surfacing by Waterloo Bridge. The subway was part of a grand urban regeneration scheme, intended to clean up the slums to the east of the Strand and to create a commercial hub on Kingsway, London's widest boulevard at the time. Named in honour of King Edward VII, Kingsway embodied the modern face of London. In the early 1930s, the tunnel was extended to accommodate the new double-decker trams, which proved to be a huge hit with the public. But the advent of the automobile soon put paid to the popularity of the tram. In the early 1950s, the tram network was dismantled. The last tram clattered through Kingsway on 5 July 1952.

In 1964, part of the tunnel was converted into the Strand underpass to ease traffic congestion. The rest of the tunnel was used as a flood control centre in the 1970s, but this was closed down in 1984 when the Thames Barrier opened (see p. 220). The derelict Kingsway subway is now used to store old street signs and traffic cones. Although attempts to convert it into a film studio were rejected on safety grounds, the tunnel has featured in several movies, including 'Bhowani Junction' (1955) and 'The Avengers' (1998). It was put to most imaginative use in 2004 by a group of art students from Central St Martin's, who staged an exhibition called 'Thought-Crime,' inspired by George Orwell's 1984, in this spooky subterranean setting. London's authorities periodically announce plans to reinstate a tram network in the capital, but so far only the remote corners of South London have it. Whether the trams come back into town and the Kingsway subway will be revived remains to be seen.

© Tony Hisgett

04.

12–13 Lincoln's Inn Fields, WC2A 3BP
Holborn or Temple tube

CANDLELIT TOURS OF SIR JOHN SOANE'S MUSEUM

Crepuscular sepulchres

A bricklayer's son, Sir John Soane (1753-1837) rose to become one of the foremost architects of his day. He designed Dulwich Picture Gallery and the Bank of England, though many of his designs remained unbuilt – a great pity as they were often wildly eccentric, such as a proposed piazza across the Thames, supported by hundreds of columns, which would have blocked most river traffic.

Soane's own home grew exponentially with his growing collection of antiquities, art, architectural drawings and models. From 1792 to 1824, Soane demolished and rebuilt three houses overlooking Lincoln's Inn Fields to accommodate this extraordinary hoard.

The collection reflects a magpie mentality, but the overall effect is intensely personal and visually rich. There are sarcophagi and stained glass, watches and clocks, a stockpile of gems, bust-filled alcoves, sky-lit statues, and secret panels that are ceremoniously flung open by witty, white-gloved guides to reveal masterpieces by Canaletto, Turner, and Hogarth.

After the death of his wife, Soane lived alone amidst his collection, constantly adding to and rearranging it. Partly to spite his son, George, a penniless author, Soane negotiated an Act of Parliament in 1833 to bequeath the house and its contents to the nation – a museum to which 'amateurs and students in Painting, Sculpture and Architecture' should have free access, with the proviso that it should remain intact and unchanged.

Over the years, incremental changes did happen: Soane's private apartments were turned into offices, some rooms were sealed, and artifacts stowed away in a futile attempt to make the space less cluttered. Now, after a seven-year restoration, Nos. 12 and 13 have finally been returned to their original splendour, the interiors bathed in an amber glow, which the architect dubbed 'a light subdued, but not exhausted'.

Soane was fascinated with the manipulation of light and shade to create 'those fanciful effects that constitute the poetry of architecture', using coloured and stained glass, mirrors and domes, to create different moods. On the last Friday of every month, from 6–9.15pm, visitors can experience this strange and surprising trove as its owner would have done after dark – by candlelight. The over-populated collection retreats into shadow, creating a fantastically gothic atmosphere. You'll have to queue to get a look in, but it's totally worth the wait.

05.

St Etheldreda's Church, 14 Ely Place, EC1N 6RY
Chancery Lane or Farringdon tube

THE RELIC OF ST ETHELDREDA

Withered hands and sore throats

'To the public it is one of those unsatisfactory streets which lead nowhere; to the inhabitants it is quiet and pleasant; to the student of old London it is possessed of all the charms which can be given by five centuries of change and the long residence of the great and noble.' Thus wrote George Walter Thornbury of Ely Place in 1878.

Today, Ely Place remains a fascinating little cul-de-sac, guarded by a formidable gate and miniature lodge for the beadles who once patrolled the street. Every hour, beadles in top hats and greatcoats would cry out the time and a weather report to the fortunate inhabitants of the grand Georgian townhouses.

Tucked between them is St Etheldreda's, one of only two extant buildings in London built in the reign of Edward I. Built in 1250, this is the last vestige of the palace of the Bishops of Ely, whose 58 acres of orchards, vineyards and lawns stretched down to the Thames. Administered by the See of Ely, 100 miles away in Cambridgeshire, the estate was beyond the jurisdiction of the City of London – and thus much favoured by criminals on the run.

Inside the small, gothic, and rather gloomy church, among the martyrs of the Reformation, is a creepy relic of its patron, St Etheldreda. A fragment of her uncorrupted pale white hand, donated to the church in the 19th century, is kept in a jewel casket to the right of the high altar. Removed in Norman times, her hand was hidden during the persecution of Catholics on the Duke of Norfolk's estate.

The tasty strawberries from St Etheldreda's garden are mentioned in Shakespeare's 'Richard III'.

Henry VIII and his first wife Catherine of Aragon binged at a five-day feast in the crypt of St Etheldreda in 1531.

THE BLESSING OF SORE THROATS

As well as patron saint of chastity (she died a virgin, despite being married twice), Etheldreda is believed to cure sore throats. She died of the plague in 679, blaming the tumour on her neck on her sinful fondness for fancy necklaces. In February, on the day of St Blaise (apparently, he was sainted for saving a child from choking to death on a fishbone), people with throat and neck infections flock to St Etheldreda to be anointed with two lit candles that are tied together.

06.

Ye Olde Mitre, Ely Court (between Hatton Garden and Ely Place), EC1N 6SJ
Chancery Lane or Farringdon tube

THE CHERRY TREE AT THE MITRE TAVERN

Quaint vestige of an Elizabethan feud

Just off Hatton Garden, London's jewellery district, is Ely Court, where Ye Olde Mitre is hidden. The pub's largely intact 18th-century interior is split into three small rooms downstairs, one of which, known as Ye Closet, is large enough to hold a table surrounded by benches and nothing more. Best of all, there is no piped music or fruit machines, a far rarer thing in London pubs than might be imagined.

Inside a glass case in the front bar is the preserved remains of a cherry tree trunk – the land on which the pub was built was originally part of the garden of Ely Palace, property of the Bishop of Ely (see p. 70). In 1576, Elizabeth I's favourite, Christopher Hatton, finagled his way into possession of the site, with the connivance of the queen and against the wishes of the bishop. The cherry tree marked the dividing line where, like two teenagers sharing a bedroom, the two men split the garden. Legend has it that the queen danced the maypole around the tree, but this smells of Merrie England wishful thinking.

Other notable pub interiors nearby include the Blackfriar on Queen Victoria Street. The latter's marble and copper interior is decorated with bas-reliefs of jolly monks, and there's a barrel-vaulted snug lined with mottoes such as 'Finery is Foolery' and 'Wisdom is Rare', presumably there for the pleasure of more lugubrious drinkers.

FULLER'S
YE OLDE MITRE

07.

West Smithfield, EC1A 9DS
Barbican, Farringdon or St Paul's tube

SECRETS OF ST BARTHOLOMEW'S THE GREATER

Bad puns, briny floods

Very little of early medieval London remains intact today, because Londoners, like the unwise little pig, built houses of wood, and the city burned down in 1077, 1087, 1132, 1136, 1203, 1212, 1220 and 1227. Almost anything left intact from these was destroyed in the Great Fire of 1666. This church is a rare survivor, despite having suffered from Zeppelin bombing in World War I and the Blitz in World War II. It was also occupied by squatters in the 18th century. The Lady Chapel was used as a commercial property; Benjamin Franklin served a year there as a journeyman printer.

Inside, the crossing and choir are mostly Norman, with round arching and massive decorated pillars; these muffle sound and light, creating a grey, crepuscular atmosphere. Notable features include the tomb of Rahere, founder of the church. Opposite this is an oriel window into an oratory, or semi-private chapel, for a wealthy Prior named Bolton. The window is decorated with Bolton's rebus, a visual pun depicting the symbol of a barrel pierced by an arrow (a bolt plus a tun, meaning barrel). There's also the bust of Edward Cooke made of 'weeping marble'. This used to cry if the weather was wet enough; nowadays, unfortunately, central heating has dried out the stone. The inscription beneath the statue still exhorts visitors to 'unsluice your briny floods'.

Bart's remains connected to the hospital across the street that was founded at the same time. Within the hospital is a smaller church, called (naturally) Bartholomew the Lesser. The hospital also has a small museum), whose crowning glory is an unusual pair of large murals by William Hogarth depicting the Good Samaritan and the Christ at the pool of Bethesda. Hogarth allegedly painted them for free in order to prevent an Italian getting his hands on the job.

© Diliff

The church has historic links with the 'Worshipful Companies' of London. These include traditional professions such as The Haberdashers' Company, The Butchers' Company and The Fletchers' Company (a guild for arrow makers), as well as modern ones like the Information Technologists' Company, the Tax Advisors' Company, and the Guild of Public Relations Practitioners.

08.

Holborn Viaduct, EC1A 2DQ
St Paul's or Chancery Lane tube, Farringdon tube or rail, City Thameslink rail

THE EXECUTIONER'S BELL OF ST SEPULCHRE-WITHOUT-NEWGATE

For whom the death bell tolls

St Sepulchre Church is one of the 'cockney bells' of London. It's immortalized in the nursery rhyme 'Oranges and Lemons' as the 'bells of Old Bailey', the nickname for the Central Criminal Court across the road. The latter was formerly the site of the infamous Newgate prison (see p. 82), thankfully demolished in 1902. This rather plain church was rebuilt after the Great Fire, but subsequently butchered by the Victorians. The odd name refers to the church's position outside London Wall, specifically at Newgate, which was the north-western entrance to the City.

The area between the prison and church became London's execution ground when the gallows was moved from Tyburn in 1783. Eighteenth-century London law was bloodthirsty. Over 350 crimes were punishable by death, but by 1861 only treason, piracy, mutiny and murder were capital offences. Public executions were still hugely popular events – in 1840, Charles Dickens witnessed one along with 40,000 other spectators, including William Thackeray – but in 1868, the gallows was moved inside the prison.

The tenor bell at St Sepulchre-without-Newgate was rung for an impending execution. The hand-held 'execution bell', still in the church, was also rung between the 17th and 19th centuries. A clerk would pace outside the cells of the condemned, ringing the bell and reciting the following 'wholesome advice' three times:

Prepare you, for tomorrow you will die.
Watch all, and pray, the hour is drawing near
That you before th' Almighty must appear.
Examine well yourselves, in time repent,
That you may not t' eternal flames be sent;
And when St Sepulchre's bell tomorrow tolls,
The Lord have mercy on your souls!

A pious, or possibly ghoulish, merchant named Robert Dove gave £40 to the parish in 1604 to ensure that this gruesome ritual was performed in perpetuity.

BOUQUETS AT THE OLD BAILEY

Trials at the Old Bailey are open to the public, but you cannot reserve a seat. Queuing for the public gallery starts at about 9.30am. A list of trials is published outside the main gate; Court One is generally where the most notorious trials are set. One tradition that has survived since the Old Bailey was located in the grounds of Newgate prison is that the judges carry a bunch of flowers at the start of each session, a practice initiated as a feeble attempt to mask the noxious stench from the cells.

The Newgate Execution Bell

09.

Cock Lane and Giltspur Street, EC1A 9DD
St Paul's tube, Farringdon tube or rail

THE GOLDEN BOY OF PYE CORNER

Glutton who got the rap for the Great Fire

High above the corner of Cock Lane and Giltspur Street is a gilded statue of a fat little boy that marks the limits of the Great Fire of London.

The Golden Boy was erected to put an end to the conflicting theories surrounding the cause of the Great Fire. At first, the Fire was blamed on a deranged French silversmith called Robert Hubert after he made a confession. He was promptly executed, but it was later discovered that he had arrived in the country two days after the fire started. William Lilly, a famous astrologer who predicted a fire the year before, almost went to the scaffold with the unfortunate Hubert, but talked his way out of it in front of a special committee at the House of Commons.

The Catholics were the next to get the rap. Eventually, the City Elders decided to blame the fire on the sin of gluttony. To make their point, they inscribed the pudgy effigy thus: 'The Boy at Pye Corner was erected to commemorate the staying of the Great Fire which beginning at Pudding Lane was ascribed to the sin of gluttony when not attributed to the Papists as on the Monument, and the Boy was made prodigiously fat to enforce the moral.'

The site of the Golden Boy used to be home to The Fortunes of War, a pub favoured by 'resurrection men' who sold corpses to the anatomists at St Bartholomew's hospital over the road. The corpses – fresh from the road, the river, or occasionally the grave – were exhibited in an upstairs room by the landlord, labelled with the finder's name.

THE ONLY PUBLIC STATUE OF HENRY VIII IN LONDON

Further down the street, another prodigiously fat boy is immortalised in stone. Henry VIII, at his most whale-like, glowers above the Henry Gate entrance to St Bartholomew's Hospital. Topped with a strange little crown and wearing a codpiece that draws the eye, this is the only public statue of Henry VIII in London.

PUCKRIDGE. Fecit

10.

Corner of Giltspur Street and Holborn Viaduct, EC1A 2DQ
St Paul's tube, Farringdon tube/rail, City Thameslink rail

LONDON'S FIRST DRINKING FOUNTAIN

Replace the cup

As well as an execution site for heretics and dissidents, Smithfield meat market was once a slaughterhouse. The anxious herds awaiting the butcher's blade were at least granted a drink of water at the cattle trough on West Smithfield. The trough bears the logo of the Metropolitan Drinking Fountain and Cattle Trough Association, 'the only agency for providing free supplies of water for man and beast in the streets of London', according to early advertisements. The association was established in 1859 by Samuel Gurney, an MP alarmed by the insalubrious quality of London's drinking water after Dr John Snow (see p. 42) had identified it as the source of a cholera outbreak. Down the road from Smithfield, on the corner of Giltspur Street and Holborn Viaduct, is London's first drinking fountain. It's an inconspicuous red granite memorial to Gurney's philanthropy, set into the railings of St Sepulchre Church. The church was keen to be seen as a patron of the poor – and to provide an antidote to beer.

Huge crowds gathered for the fountain's inauguration on 21 April 1859. Mrs Wilson, daughter of the Archbishop of Canterbury, was the first to taste the water from a silver cup. The filtered water came from the New River (see p. 238). The inscription urges thirsty passers-by to 'REPLACE THE CUP'. Today, in less trusting times, the two original (somewhat mildewed) metal mugs are fastened to the railings with chains. By 1870, the Drinking Fountain Association had installed 140 fountains in London. Many of them have also survived.

The Geffrye Museum contains an impression of the original fountain, which was more elaborate, painted by W.A. Atkinson in 1860.

MINIATURE BLUECOATS

On the corner of Hatton Garden and St Cross Street, embedded into the façade of an office building, stand the twee statuettes of a boy holding a cap and Bible and a girl who seems to be clutching a shopping list. These figurines, which are found across London, signal that this was once a charitable 'blewcoat' school for underprivileged girls and boys. In Tudor and Stuart times, blue clothes were the mark of the lower classes as blue was the cheapest dye available. This school, dating from 1690, was probably designed by Christopher Wren. The 18th-century figurines were stowed away in Berkshire for safekeeping during the Blitz – a wise move, as the building was damaged by bombs.

METROPOLITAN
PUBLIC DRINKING
FOUNTAIN
ERECTED ON
HOLBORN HILL
IN 1859 AND
REMOVED WHEN THE
VIADUCT WAS
CONSTRUCTED IN
1867.
PLACE THE

11.

Beneath the Viaduct Tavern, 126 Newgate Street, EC1A 7AA
St Paul's tube, City Thameslink rail

NEWGATE CELLS

Not your average cellar

Eighteenth- and nineteenth-century London was obsessed with imprisonment and punishment. Capital crimes included impersonating an Egyptian (a gypsy), stealing an heiress, or poaching a rabbit, and as a result punishment centres flourished. Tate Britain is built on the site of Millbank prison, which was eventually closed because inmates tiresomely kept dying.

Little remains of the infamous Newgate Prison, the city's main jail for almost five centuries. Originally located by a medieval gate in the Roman London Wall, it was extended over the years, and remained in use between 1188 and 1902, with its last incarnation built in an 'architecture terrible' style intended to discourage law-breaking. The Central Criminal Courts now stand on the site. However, if you go into the Viaduct Tavern and ask nicely when it's not too busy, the staff will show you cells that survived the prison's closure.

The underground cells still look like the real deal. Although the pub owners have hung prints in the passage down to the cells, there is no suggestion of a tourist recreation. One of the cells is popular with ghost hunters, but you don't need to be psychic to sniff out the misery. The cells are genuinely horrible: cold, damp and dark. Up to 20 criminals – usually debtors – were crammed into each one. There was no toilet; one jailer described the stench as being bad enough to choke a horse. The only daylight came from a tube leading to street level, used by relatives or sympathetic passers-by to drop down scraps of food. Because prisons were privately run, prisoners had to pay for the privilege of being locked up – or starve to death.

Wealthy prisoners could opt for private cells, complete with regular visits from prostitutes. Even more grisly is the old cell for the condemned across the road at the Old Bailey. This was larger than normal cells, as those waiting to be hanged received more visitors. The corridor leading from the cell to the scaffold is increasingly narrow, making it harder for the condemned to turn and run. A sinister example of form and function in architecture.

In contrast, the Viaduct Tavern itself is a beautiful Victorian pub, with a wrought copper ceiling and a triptych of oils representing the four statues of Commerce, Agriculture, Science and Fine Arts on nearby Holborn Viaduct. The floor above allegedly housed an opium den in the 19th century.

12.

Postman's Park, King Edward Street, EC1A 7BT
St Paul's or Barbican tube

POSTMAN PARK

The memorial to heroic self-sacrifice

Thrillingly gruesome or horribly sad (or just plain horrible) depending on your point of view, these memorials line one side of Postman's Park, named after the General Post Office on its southern boundary. Set up by G.F. Watts and unveiled in 1900 for Queen Victoria's Jubilee, they memorialise fatal acts of heroism by ordinary Londoners.

The descriptions of these acts are full-blooded, with lots of children, burning, drowning, and train accidents. The earliest death commemorated was pantomime artiste Sarah Smith, who 'died of terrible injuries received when attempting in her inflammable dress to extinguish the flames which had enveloped her companion' in 1863. Eight-year-old Henry Bristow is the youngest, who 'saved his little sister's life by tearing off her flaming clothes but caught fire himself and died of burns and shock'. John Cranmer Cambridge 'was drowned near Ostend whilst saving the life of a stranger and a foreigner', presumably the same person.

The thought, or hope, of heroism like this is pleasing. The ceramics of the memorial are a homely counterpoint to the marble statues of war heroes in the capital. The glazed tiles, bearing decorative motifs reminiscent of William Morris, were made at the famous Doulton factory, still in operation today.

Watts hoped to see similar memorials erected in every town in England. Ever the optimist, he left lots of space on the walls of the park so people could continue to put up tablets. He died in 1904, passing the running of the memorial over to his wife Alice. By the time she died, only 53 of the planned 120 tiles were completed. However, in 2009, the first new tile in 78 years was unveiled: 'Leigh Pitt, Reprographic Operator, Aged 30, saved a drowning boy from the canal at Thamesmead, but sadly was unable to save himself'.

ENGLAND'S MICHELANGELO

Watts, a noted Victorian painter dubbed 'England's Michelangelo,' was outspokenly socialist. He declared in a letter to the Times of London that 'the national prosperity of a Nation is not an abiding possession, the deeds of its people are.' This progressive ideology was the inspiration for his memorial.

P·C·PERCY EDWIN COOK
METROPOLITAN POLICE
VOLUNTARILY DESCENDED HIGH
TENSION CHAMBER AT KENSINGTON
TO RESCUE TWO WORKMEN
OVERCOME BY POISONOUS GAS
7·OCT·1927·
·HERBERT MACONOGHU·
SCHOOL BOY FROM WIMBLEDON AGED 13
HIS PARENTS ABSENT IN INDIA, LOST
HIS LIFE IN VAINLY TRYING TO RESCUE
·HIS TWO SCHOOL FELLOWS WHO WERE·
DROWNED AT GLOVERS POOL, CROYDE,
NORTH DEVON • AUGUST·28·1882·
JAMES HEWERS·
ON SEPT·24·1878
WAS KILLED BY A TRAIN
AT RICHMOND IN THE
ENDEAVOUR TO SAVE
ANOTHER MAN·

13.

Panyer Alley, EC1M 8AD
St Paul's tube

THE BREAD BASKET BOY

An enigmatic statue

Smokers huddled outside Café Nero and commuters dashing in and out of St Paul's tube station are oblivious to the naked boy perched on a bread basket who watches over them, proffering what appears to be a bunch of grapes.

Beneath this little stone relief is a weathered inscription: 'When ye have sought the citty round yet still this is the highest ground. August the 27, 1688'. This couplet does not make much sense in reference to its current location, a decidedly flat passage running between the tube station and St Paul's churchyard; however, the statue originally stood in Paternoster Row. When the building on which he sat was demolished in 1892, the boy was moved to Farrows Bank on Cheapside as its mascot. The baker boy's luck must have run out, because the bank folded in 1930.

In 1964, the statue was moved to this innocuous alley, which was once the centre of London's baking business. Panyer Alley was named after the boys who sold their wares from baskets, or panniers, after a law was passed in the 14th century forbidding the sale of bread in bakers' houses; it could only be sold in the king's markets. Bakers bypassed the law by selling loaves in baskets on the streets. As commuters rush past, croissants in hand, they should spare a thought for the bread peddlers of bygone years.

WHEN YV HAVE SOVGHT
THE CITTY ROVND
YET STILL THS IS
THE HIGHST GROVND
AVGVST THE 27
1688

14.

17 Gough Square, EC4A 3DE
Blackfriars, Temple, Holborn or Chancery Lane tube. City Thameslink, Blackfriars or Farringdon rail

DR JOHNSON'S HOUSE

Home to a harmless drudge

London loves Dr Johnson, who confirmed the superiority of the place: 'You find no man, at all intellectual, who is willing to leave London. No, Sir, when a man is tired of London, he is tired of life; for there is in London all that life can afford'.

However, like most people living here, 'Dictionary' Johnson wasn't a native, but from the Midlands city of Lichfield. He arrived in London in 1737 aged 28, after a disastrous career as a schoolteacher. He scraped a living for the next thirty years writing biographies, poetry, essays, pamphlets and parliamentary reports, and most famously his dictionary, which he compiled in the garret of this house in Gough Square. It took him nearly nine years to complete all 42,773 entries, with the help of five or six assistants. Perhaps it took so long because Johnson, who defined a lexicographer as 'a harmless drudge', rarely got out of bed before noon.

The house, where Johnson lived between 1748 and 1759, is a little hard to find among the surrounding maze of courtyards and passages. It is one of the few remnants of Georgian London left in the City. Built in 1700, it fell into disarray and was used variously as a hotel, a print shop, and a storehouse, until it was eventually acquired in 1911 by MP Cecil Harmsworth, who restored and opened it to the public. The lovely, delicate interior is characteristic of the era, with panelled rooms and a collection of period furniture, prints and portraits. The Curator's House next door is allegedly the smallest residential building in the Square Mile.

Dr Johnson was famously fond of cats. There is a statue of Hodge, his black cat, in the square outside the house, perched on a dictionary beside a couple of empty oyster shells. Johnson would go out personally to buy oysters for his favourite feline, rather than risk his servants resenting the cat if they were dispatched to fetch his supper.

JOHN WILKES, RAKE AND RADICAL

Johnson didn't choose this house by accident. It lies close to Fetter Lane and Fleet Street, historically London's hotbed of journalism. On Fetter Lane, look out for the flattering statue of Johnson's contemporary John Wilkes, an incendiary radical, journalist and politician who was famously hideous but also had a rake's reputation (he claimed it 'took him only half an hour to talk away his face'). Wilkes' writing made him many enemies in the monarchy and government, yet thanks to popular support he was largely able to resist imprisonment.

15.

Fleet Street, EC4Y 8AU
Blackfriars tube

THE CHARNEL HOUSE AT ST BRIDE'S

Down among the dead men

St Bride's, at the bottom of Fleet Street, has a number of claims to fame. Widely known as the Journalists' Church, its tiered spire was also the prototype for the modern wedding cake: local baker Thomas Rich made a pile of money with the design from his nearby bakery on Ludgate Hill.

The current church, reckoned to be the eighth version, is a Wren design that was bombed out in the Blitz, and then rebuilt using clear glass and less furniture. This means the interior is lighter and airier than most Wren churches in the capital.

When Wren rebuilt using the footprint of the previous church, he raised the floor level and added a crypt where the wealthier parishioners could be buried. This is now a museum, mostly of the history of the church and its links with Fleet Street. There is some medieval stained glass, an iron coffin designed to deter grave robbers, and allegedly you can hear the buried river Fleet flowing nearby, but if you take the guided tour you get to see the spooky stuff.

St Bride's still has its charnel house. These were repositories of old bones from the churchyard that were tidied away in preparation for the Resurrection. Almost all of the bones in the house are skulls and long bones, so presumably God will fill in the gaps when the trumpets sound and the dead rise. They were moved to make room for fresh burials; unless you were wealthy enough to pay for burial in the church, you'd eventually end up here. It was possible to hurry the process – Samuel Pepys paid to have bones moved from the churchyard so his brother could be buried somewhere nice. The practice only stopped with the arrival of coffin burials, which drastically slowed decomposition and led to rapid overcrowding; before this, everyone was buried in a shroud and returned to the earth at speed. The church has a bone collection from the crypt burials, all in individual cardboard boxes with disconcerting labels like 'skull', 'mandible', 'hair'.

The church is also well known for its music and has an excellent choir and organist.

THEY WOULD BUILD A PUB FOR THEMSELVES

Right next to the churchyard is a pub called the Old Bell Tavern, which from Fleet Street doesn't look that special, but in fact, has a lovely old interior from the same era as the church. Apparently, whenever workmen started on a Wren church, they would build a pub for themselves before anything else. Admirable stuff.

CHURCH-WARDENS 1827
THIS TABLET
IS INSCRIBED
TO THE MEMORY OF
ROBERT OBBARD Esq.
FORMERLY OF THIS PARISH
WHO DEPARTED THIS LIFE
AT HIS RESIDENCE IN THE PARAGON
BLACKHEATH
AGED 83 YEARS
A MEMBER OF THE COURT OF
SACRED
TO THE HONOURED MEMORY OF
WALTER JOHN PICKET
AND TO THE GOVERNING BODY
OF THE ST BRIDE FOUNDATION
THIS MARBLE IS PLACED HERE
IN GRATEFUL RECOGNITION OF THE
QUALITIES OF MIND AND CHARACT
WHICH HE UNSPARINGLY
DEVOTED TO HIS WORK

SAFETY FOR THE DEAD!
Approbation of the Board of Works.
FUNERALS FURNISHED.

16.

Two Temple Place, WC2R 3BD
Temple tube

TWO TEMPLE PLACE

Astor's inner sanctum

This mansion overlooking Victoria Embankment only recently opened to the public on a regular basis. Next to Middle Temple, you could easily mistake it for an extension of the Inns of Court. Though undeniably impressive, the crenellated Portland stone façade looks almost plain compared to the elaborate craftsmanship inside. A clue to the original owner sails above the roof: a golden weathervane of the Santa Maria, the ship on which Columbus set sail to 'discover' America.

Completed in 1895, this was the estate office of William Waldorf Astor, one of the world's richest men. When Astor quit New York for London, he wanted an HQ that reflected his status, ancestry and personal passions. He persuaded John Loughborough Pearson to take on the project, with the promise of 'a free hand to erect a perfect building irrespective of cost'. Pearson blew £250,000 (equivalent to £10 million today) of Astor's fortune. It was money well spent.

The front door is lit by two bronze lamps, draped with cherubs chatting on the telephone and waving light bulbs, an allusion to the new-fangled apparatus inside. A hybrid of Tudor, Gothic Revivalist and Renaissance styles, the interior works surprisingly well. From the floor inlaid with coloured marble and precious stones to the stained glass skylight, the Staircase Hall takes your breath away. The mahogany balustrade is punctuated by statues of Astor's literary heroes, the Three Musketeers. On the landing, ten ebony columns support carved scenes from Shakespeare and American classics like The Scarlet Letter and The Last of the Mohicans.

Astor's oak-panelled library is fitted with secret cupboards and a hidden door so that he could surprise visitors in the meeting room. 'Ornamental' is an understatement. There's a medieval hammer-beam ceiling, twin inglenooks decorated with stained-glass landscapes, and a gilded frieze of 50 of Astor's favourite real and fictional characters, from Machiavelli to Martin Luther.

Like Scrooge McDuck, Astor kept bags of gold sovereigns in three different strongrooms. After his wife died, Astor slept in a four-poster bed next to the safe. Though intensely private and pernickety, Astor was desperate to infiltrate the British aristocracy. He donated vast sums to charity and the Conservative Party. His generosity paid off: two years before he died, he became Lord Astor.

Now owned by The Bulldog Trust, an incubator for charities, Two Temple Place hosts excellent winter exhibitions drawn from the collections of regional British galleries and museums.

17.

216 Strand, WC2R 1AP
Temple tube

TWININGS TEA MUSEUM

Teapots and tips

Drinking tea may be as quintessentially British as sinking pints on a Friday night, but the tradition of taking tea originated in China back in 2737 BCE. This heritage is hinted at in the exotic façade of Twinings tea shop on the Strand, with the figures of two Chinamen draped over the doorway.

Thomas Twining bought Tom's Coffee House in 1706 on a site behind the existing shop. Ironically, tea was first introduced to London society at the city's disreputable coffee houses. Competition between the coffee houses was fierce, with fresh ideas needed to keep the business alive. The difference at Tom's was tea, although Twinings still stocks coffee among the packets of Earl Grey and English Breakfast. With success came expansion. By 1717, Thomas had acquired three adjacent houses and converted them into the shop that stands on the Strand today.

Thankfully, prices have dropped since the early 18th century, when tea cost the equivalent of £160 for 100g. At the back of this fragrant little shop, fetchingly decorated with portraits of the Twinings dynasty through the ages, is a small museum. The collection includes a copy of Queen Victoria's Royal Warrant from 1837 (Twinings has supplied every successive British monarch since), antique tea caddies, invoices and advertisements. The most remarkable exhibit is a plain wooden box bearing the initials T.I.P. – short for 'To Insure Promptness'. Patrons of coffee-houses would drop a few pennies into these boxes to encourage swifter service – the origins of the modern-day 'tip'.

If you'd like to go deeper into tea, Twinings opened a Loose Tea Bar at their flagship store in 2013. It offers a variety of masterclasses and tasting sessions that include the etiquette of taking tea in the UK. Call the store to book.

TWININGS
EST. 1706
bodum
TWININGS

18.

Royal College of Surgeons, 38–43 Lincoln's Inn Fields, WC2A 3PE
Holborn tube

HUNTERIAN MUSEUM

Frankenstein's torture chamber

Originally part of the medieval guild of Barber-Surgeons, the Royal College of Surgeons houses two museums: the Wellcome Museum (only open to medical practitioners and students), and the Hunterian, based on the eminent 18th-century surgeon John Hunter's gruesome collection of comparative anatomy and pathology specimens.

Hunter started out as an assistant in the anatomy school of his elder brother, William. A fast learner with a knack for the dissection of the dead, John Hunter developed new treatments for common ailments such as gunshot wounds and venereal disease. An avid collector, he moved to a large house in Leicester Square in 1783, where he organised his collection into a museum. (There is still a statue of him in the square). A notorious curmudgeon, Hunter became the leading teacher of surgery of his time. Success did not mellow him: he died in 1793 after suffering a fit during an argument.

His collection was then bought by the government in 1799, and became part of the Museum of the Royal College of Surgeons when it opened in 1813. By the end of the 19th century, the museum comprised some 65,000 specimens covering anatomy and pathology, zoology, palaeontology, archaeology and anthropology. Today, the museum contains skeletons, bones, skulls and teeth; alarming wax teaching models; historic surgical and dental instruments; paintings, drawings, and sculpture. Rows of random 'things' in glass jars lend the place the atmosphere of a Frankenstein movie.

THE SKELETON OF A 7'7" GIANT

In the 18th century, surgeons were widely regarded as butchers and the museum still has one foot in the seamier past of the anatomy trade. One of the centrepieces of Hunter's collection is the skeleton of Charles O'Brien, an Irish giant who stood at 7'7' and caused a sensation at fairs and fetes nationwide. When O'Brien fell ill in 1782, Hunter haunted his sickbed. Knowing his body would be a great prize for the anatomist, O'Brien gave strict instructions that his corpse should be sealed in a lead coffin and paid some fishermen to bury him at sea. Hunter was not to be thwarted. After O'Brien's death, he paid the fishermen £500 for the corpse, which was then boiled in a copper vat so that only the bones remained. They are on display in the museum.

P1521

19.

Carting Lane, WC2R 0ET, next to The Cole Hole bar
Charing Cross, Embankment, or Temple tube

PATENT SEWER VENTILATING LAMP

The odyssey of 'Iron Lily'

Now powered by conventional household gas, the ornate lamp post opposite the stage door of the Savoy Theatre was originally designed to burn methane waste from the sewage system. The Patent Sewer Ventilating lamp was invented by J.E. Webb, who realised that 'firedamp' from London's new-fangled sewage system could be recycled as a cheap source of energy and blended with the mains gas. Equipped with a hollow post to allow waste gas from the sewers running beneath the Thames Embankment to shoot up to the flame, the sewage lamp thus fulfilled two important functions: illuminating this scruffy back alley and burning off unpleasant smells for residents at the nearby Savoy Hotel. Little did these glamorous guests realise their effluents were being used to cast light on Carting Lane (otherwise known as Farting Lane).

Webb patented his sewage lamp in 1895, and sold around 2,500 of them worldwide, but their success was limited by the risk of stinky leaks and dangerous explosions from the highly combustible gasses. In 1950, a careless lorry driver backed into the light, thus destroying one of the last vestiges of Victorian ingenuity. 'Iron Lily' was restored and operates as the standard gas lamp that you see today.

LONDON RECORDS

– London's first gaslit street: Pall Mall (1807)
– London's longest road: Western Avenue (11.3 miles)
– London's smallest square: Pickering Place (see p. 46)
– London's longest bridge: Waterloo (381 metres)
– London's narrowest street: Brydges Place (15 inches wide)

THE WRONG-WAY STREET

Savoy Lane, a tiny street running from the Strand to the entrance of the Savoy Hotel, is the only street in Britain where traffic drives on the right. A law was introduced in 1902 so that carriages and cabs dropping people off at the Savoy Theatre next door would not block the hotel's entrance. This quirk dates back to the time when hansom cabs delivered guests to the hotel, but is just as useful today when most of the moneyed guests arrive in stretch limousines or black cabs, which are too big to turn around in such tight space. Drivers have to perform a U-turn to exit the street, staying on the right-hand side.

CARTING
LANE WC2
CITY OF WESTMINSTER
SAVOY
THEATRE

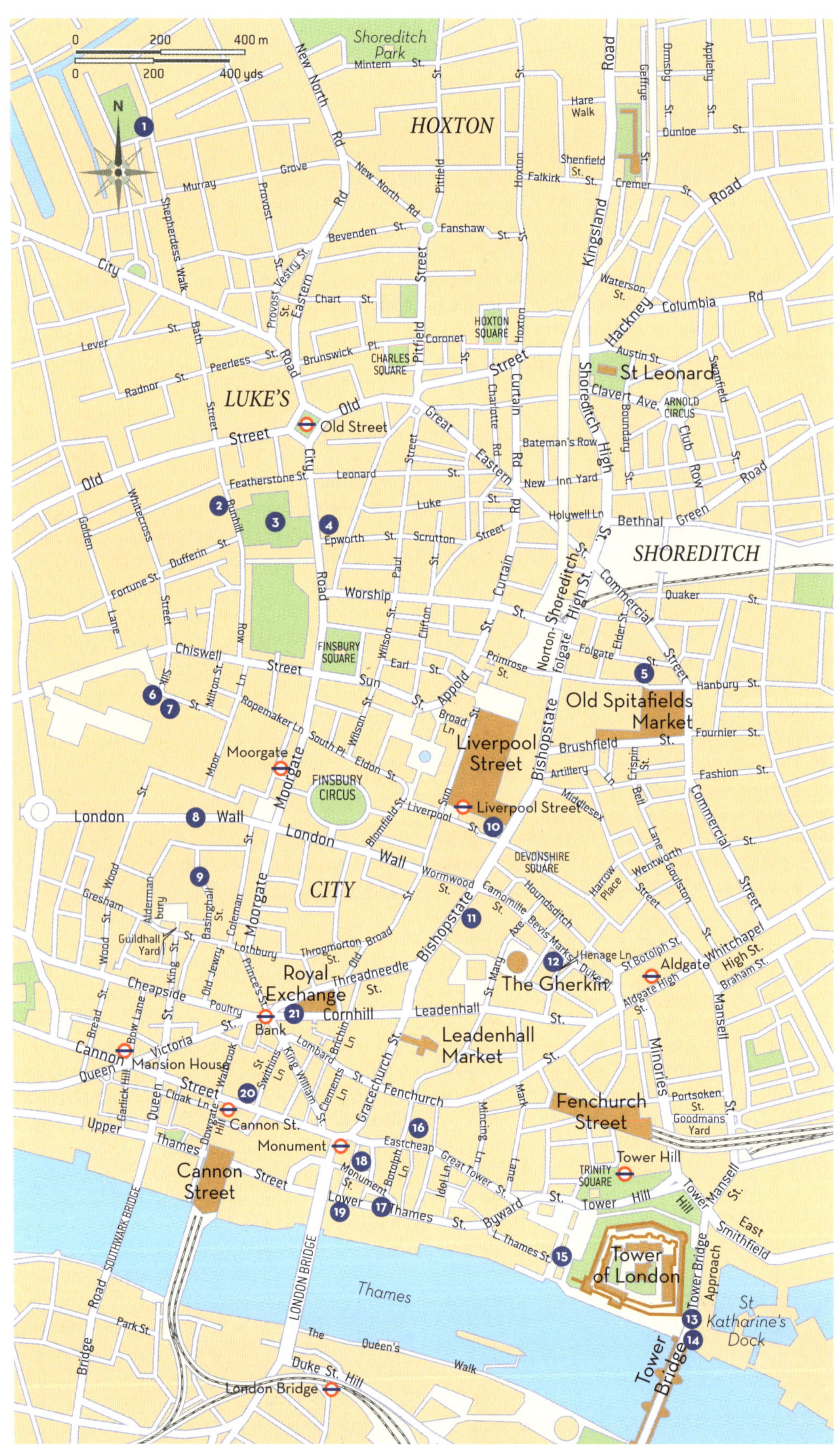
0
200
400 m
0
200
400 yds
N
Shoreditch Park
HOXTON
LUKE'S
CITY
SHOREDITCH
Old Street
Moorgate
Liverpool Street
Bank
Mansion House
Cannon Street
Monument
Aldgate
Tower Hill
London Bridge
Old Spitafields Market
Royal Exchange
The Gherkin
Leadenhall Market
Fenchurch Street
St Leonard
Tower of London
Tower Bridge
Thames
St Katharine's Dock
HOXTON SQUARE
CHARLES SQUARE
FINSBURY SQUARE
FINSBURY CIRCUS
DEVONSHIRE SQUARE
ARNOLD CIRCUS
TRINITY SQUARE
LONDON BRIDGE
SOUTHWARK BRIDGE
New North Rd
City Road
Old Street
Great Eastern St.
Kingsland Road
Hackney Road
Columbia Rd
Bethnal Green Road
Shoreditch High St.
Commercial St.
Commercial St.
Bishopsgate
London Wall
Moorgate
Cheapside
Cornhill
Threadneedle St.
Leadenhall St.
Fenchurch St.
Gracechurch St.
King William St.
Cannon St.
Queen Victoria St.
Upper Thames St.
Lower Thames St.
Eastcheap
Great Tower St.
Minories
Mansell St.
Whitechapel High St.
Tower Bridge Approach
East Smithfield
Borough High St.
Duke St. Hill
The Queen's Walk
Bridge Road
Park St.
1
2
3
4
5
6
7
8
9
10
11
12
13
14
15
16
17
18
19
20
21

SHOREDITCH TO TOWER BRIDGE

01.

Shepherdess Walk Park
Sturt Street
N1 7QD
Angel or Old Street tube

SHEPHERDESS MOSAICS

The mural to modern-day life

Carved into a small space between two houses halfway along Shepherdess Walk is a narrow alleyway leading to an ominously dark underground tunnel. Easy to miss and tempting to avoid, the tiny sign hanging above the entrance reading 'To the Mosaics' gives a clue as to what marvels await you on the other side.

Emerging from the tunnel, you'll find a large corner of Shepherdess Walk Park decorated with tiled mosaics. These mosaics appear ancient, almost as though you've stumbled onto the perfectly preserved stones of a Roman bathhouse. However, after closer inspection, certain aspects of the mosaics start to look less-than-antique: a man uses a blower on fallen tree leaves, a woman checks a smartphone as her child feeds the ducks and a young boy anticipates a Mr Whippy ice cream on a hot summer's day. These are the scenes of modern life in Hackney, not the activities of a long-lost Roman society.

The murals were commissioned by Hackney Council in 2012 as part of the London Olympics celebration. Designed by mosaicist Tessa Hunkin, they were created by a team of 150 local volunteers, many of whom were completely new to the art of mosaic-making. The project was called 'History in the Making' and was part of an initiative, thought up by Hunkin, to offer art-based community activities to those who are often socially excluded.

The first panel tells the story of the shepherdesses, the namesakes of the park. This area of Hoxton was once a rural spot where farmers used to walk their sheep in and out of the city to reach Smithfield meat market. It was also home to an old pub called the Shepherd and Shepherdess, which offered the area which is now the park to its customers as a 'pleasure garden'. The park is rightly proud of this rural association and when the mosaics were revealed in 2012, an elaborate procession involving costumed shepherdesses, shepherds, and fake sheep made its way through the town as part of the opening ceremony.

The other panels depict the four seasons of Hackney, native plants and trees, names of supporters, and individual mosaic contributions.

THE MOSAIC OF THE YEAR AWARD

In 2014 Hunkin and the team won the Mosaic of the Year award for the Shepherdess Walk Park murals, granted by the British Association for Modern Mosaics.

After completing the Shepherdess Walk Park panels, the volunteers of the Hackney Mosaic Project went on to create many more works of art which were commissioned for display all around London. A list of these mosaics is found on the project's website.

SHEPHERDESS WALK

02.

Chequer Street, EC1Y 8PD
Barbican or Moorgate tube

WOODEN PAVEMENT

One of the last surviving examples of London's old wooden pavements

At the far end of Chequer Street, at the point where it turns into Burnhill Row, is a square of pavement that is noticeably darker than the rest of the road. Pavements around London usually end up looking like a patchwork quilt as they are re-paved and filled in over the years, but this small spot is especially interesting.

Inspect it closely and you'll spot the rings of old trees moulded into the blocks. Walk along it and you'll feel that it's softer than the stone around it.

This is one of the last surviving examples of London's old wooden pavements, a remnant of the time when horses, carriages and bicycles ruled the roads.

The design of the block pavement found on Chequer Street is thought to have emerged in 14th-century Russia, but it only gained popularity in England when wood became abundant and cheap, especially in comparison to the high price of stone.

For a long time, London's streets were paved with cobbles. But as new travel technologies took over the urban centre during the Victorian age, wooden pavements became useful for quietening the racket of steel-rimmed carriage wheels on stone, as well as protecting the horses' iron shoes from the uneven cobbled streets.

Wooden roads were not found everywhere: they were usually only laid in areas where the street noise was expected to be particularly annoying to residents. Chequer Street once had an infant school for boys and girls, which explains why they would want quieter wooden paving at the entrance.

Wood became less suitable with the arrival of the motor car. It also became quickly apparent that wooden pavements were difficult to maintain and could get extremely slippery on London's many rainy days. Business owners realised they were basically paying a 'mud tax' – they forfeited profits lost during the rainy season when the wet wooden roads became impassable.

After the Second World War most of these roads were taken up, removed and replaced with asphalt or granite. Many of the wooden blocks used as pavements were hastily stolen by local residents to be burnt in their home fires, so hardly any material evidence of the old pavements remains.

OTHER EXAMPLES OF WOODEN PAVEMENTS

Other examples of wooden pavements can be found on Belvedere Road, SE1 7GQ and Colliers Wood, SW19 2BH.

03.

38 City Rd, EC1Y 2BG
Old Street tube/rail

BUNHILL FIELDS

Deliverance for dissenters

Bunhill Fields is the site of a small graveyard to the north of the old City Wall. Bunhill supposedly derives from Bone Hill: around the year 1549, the charnel house (or bone deposit) of St Paul's was cleared for new burials, and over a thousand cartloads of bones were dumped here, on what was damp, marshy ground – enough to provide foundations for three new windmills.

In 1665, the City of London Corporation decided to use the land as a burial ground for those who could not be buried in conventional churchyards, primarily plague victims. Enclosing walls for the cemetery were built, but it seems to have never been consecrated and as a result became popular with Nonconformist Protestants who practiced outside the orthodoxy of the Church of England.

Catholic and Jewish Londoners who could afford the fees were also buried there. The list of burials in this small yard reads like a who's who of dissenters in London intellectual life – the visionary poet and painter William Blake, 'Robinson Crusoe' author Daniel Defoe, anti-slavery philanthropist Thomas Fowell Buxton, and poet and hymn-writer Isaac Watts are the most noted examples. The London poet Robert Southey called it the 'Campo Santo of the Dissenters'.

The Fields were filled with 120,000 graves before being closed in 1853. Most of the graves are fenced off, but an on-site curator will happily escort you around any of them.

ABNEY PARK CEMETERY

In 1840, Nonconformist burials were moved to Abney Park in Stoke Newington, another graveyard well worth a visit – one of the original seven cemeteries circling London that include Nunhead and Kensal Green (see p. 282 and 144). The entrance to Abney Park is built in the Egyptian Revival style – a conscious decision, as it was the first cemetery in Europe explicitly designated as nondenominational, or with 'no invidious dividing lines,' according to the group of Nonconformists led by George Collison who founded it. The most famous internees are Catherine and William Booth, founders of the Salvation Army, but large numbers of abolitionists and 19th-century missionaries are typical residents. The overgrown park is full of mature woods now. It also contains one of the two UXBs (unexploded bombs) known in Stoke Newington, so don't go digging any holes!

04.

49 City Road, EC1Y 1AU
Old Street or Moorgate tube

JOHN WESLEY'S HOUSE

The Venerable Crapper

'The world is my parish' pronounces the statue of John Wesley, founder of Methodism, in the courtyard of Wesley Chapel, a welcome refuge from the thrum of City Road. During his 88 years, Wesley lived up to his word, travelling a quarter of a million miles on horseback to deliver some 40,000 sermons.

From 1779 until his death in 1791, Wesley spent his winters in the compact Georgian townhouse beside the chapel. Though simple to the point of severity by today's standards, Wesley's three-storey home was fitted with all mod cons – wallpaper, built-in cupboards, and a fireplace in every room. New-fangled furniture included a 'cock fighting chair', to be straddled like a modern massage chair, with an adjustable easel for reading and writing. The bureau has secret compartments where Wesley hid correspondence from his jealous wife, Mary Vazielle.

Wesley was fond of his Chamber Horse, precursor of the exercise bike, a tall wooden chair with a springy seat that simulates riding a horse. Apparently, 'the vigorous bouncing would stimulate the liver'. Another example of Wesley's fascination with 'Primitive Physick' is the Electrical Machine, which administered electric shocks to cure depression, migraine, and all manner of ailments. Wesley did not try this out himself until he had experimented with his flock for a good three years. Downstairs are a few of Wesley's personal possessions including a pair of 'straights', buckled shoes that could be worn on either foot, and his 'laptop' – a wooden writing case with quills and ink, which he would balance on his saddle, composing sermons as he trotted through the countryside.

In Wesley's day, the house had no running water. His chamber pot was concealed in a wooden box in his bedroom. But in 1899, Methodist ministers installed a fine set of gentlemen's toilets to serve the congregation at the chapel, which are miraculously intact. With their red-mottled marble urinals and a dressing room with frosted-glass partitions, these public conveniences must have been the height of Victorian hygiene. The mahogany cubicles contain original Thomas Crapper toilets, their rims imprinted with 'The Venerable' in red letters. The porcelain handle on the chain instructs users to: 'Pull and let go'.

A MUSEUM OF METHODISM

In the crypt of John Wesley's Chapel next door is a small Museum of Methodism, which tells the history of this faction of the Anglican church, aimed at social outcasts and taught mainly by itinerant preachers.

© Graham Portlock and Aisha Al-Sadie

© Graham Portlock and Aisha Al-Sadie

05.

18 Folgate Street, E1 6BX
Liverpool Street tube/rail

DENNIS SEVERS' HOUSE

Still life

One house stands out among the spruce Georgian terraces of Folgate Street. With its flaming lantern and cutout silhouettes framed by crimson shutters, number 18 seems strangely detached from the commercial throb of nearby Bishopsgate, where City traders scurry about their business. When Dennis Severs, a Canadian artist, bought this ten-room house in the late 1970s, Spitalfields was a slum. He filled his dilapidated home with chipped antiques and anonymous portraits picked up from flea markets, determined to recreate an authentic 18th-century household. Armed with a candle and bedpan, Severs slept in every room, soaking up the energy and imagining the lives of its previous inhabitants. Gradually, these imaginary companions took shape as the Jervis family, Huguenot silk-weavers whose make-believe lives became an elaborate 'still life drama' for visitors to explore.

Although Severs died in 1999, visitors can still immerse themselves in his decaying fantasy world. Each room is designed to evoke a moment in time as experienced by successive generations of the Jervises from 1724 to 1914. The experience is an assault on the senses where every object is apparently charged with hidden meaning – not just a visual overload, but also the smells of ginger biscuits and mulled wine, the sounds of horse hooves, church bells, and whispered snatches of conversation. The effect is deliberately theatrical as you follow a trail of clues that suggest the ghostly presence of the Jervis clan – a half-eaten boiled egg and soldiers, a black cat asleep on an unmade bed, and what appears to be a chamber pot full of pee.

There is social commentary, too. In the gloomy servants' quarters, soiled white undergarments are strung between cobwebs, a blackened pot of mouldy cabbage sits beside a filthy hearth, and gunshots sound a death knell. It all conjures up a deeply bleak existence.

Sadly, the compelling atmosphere is punctured by patronising notes telling patrons to shut up and use their imagination. For example: 'A visit requires the same style of concentration as does an Old Masters exhibition, and a most absurd but commonly made error is to assume that it might be either amusing or appropriate for children.'

A young man still lives in the attic. Well, someone has to feed the cat and canaries.

06.

Barbican Centre, Silk Street, EC2Y 8DS
Barbican tube

BARBICAN CONSERVATORY

Urban hothouse

This tropical garden is hidden in London's brutalist landmark. As you approach the Barbican from Silk Street, a greenhouse comes into view. The lushness of the conservatory – which contains over 2,000 species of trees and plants, as well as tropical finches, quails, and exotic fish – is thrown into vibrant contrast by the surrounding glass, steel and raw concrete.

The main difficulty in visiting this garden in the sky is its limited opening times. When it was inaugurated in 1982, the conservatory was permanently open to everyone; but feeble public response saw the Corporation of the City of London whittle away visiting hours. It is now mainly used for private parties, but there are regular tours and you can even have afternoon tea in the conservatory on occasional Sundays (though you have to book in advance). Many of the ingredients, including lavender, dill, avocado and turmeric, are grown on the spot or on the surrounding estate. The conservatory itself is wrapped around the fly tower (from where scenery is lowered onto the stage below) of the Barbican's main theatre.

Low visitor response has bedevilled the Barbican since it opened. It forms part of the Barbican Estate, a hermetically sealed island within the city. Navigating the estate and the Centre is often bewildering, as the seemingly endless walkways and blank concrete walls can disorient newcomers. Even the entrances to the performance spaces are low key, certainly in comparison to traditional theatres like the Haymarket or Drury Lane.

The Barbican Estate has enjoyed a renaissance in recent years. Originally constructed for workers in the Corporation, the retro design, central location and cohesive urban system of the estate meant that when London flooded with money in the 1980s, flats were snapped up by City workers. A fashion for modernism means that London's original distaste for the estate has turned around, and it is now listed. If you can't get into the conservatory, take one of the excellent architecture tours (barbican.org.uk).

© Henry Kellner

07.

The City of London Corporation Car Park, Barbican, EC2V 5DY
Barbican tube

THE WALL OF THE CITY OF LONDON CORPORATION CAR PARK

The Roman wall in an underground carpark

A search for a parking space in the City of London Corporation's carpark can uncover some surprising things. Towards the very end of the underground garage, hiding behind column number 52, is a crumbling two-thousand-year-old wall taking up at least four valuable parking spaces. This ancient defensive structure was built by the Romans when they occupied Britain, and it is now protected and preserved by the City of London.

London was the capital city of Roman Britain. The borders of this city named 'Londinium' were defined by a 2-mile stone wall reaching from Tower Hill to Blackfriars. Some remnants of this impressive construction are easy to spot, it humps out of the ground at random points around the city, giving us an easy glimpse of the ancient gatehouses, archers slits, and turrets that were once a familiar sight to the people of Londinium. One particularly ostentatious section – Roman Fort Gate – is nearby, at 150 London Wall (EC2Y 5HN).

The Corporation carpark's wall, however, was only discovered by delving far below ground in 1957 when construction for the carpark began. Initially, this section of the wall was longer, but unfortunately the demolition required to build the carpark meant that a lot of the fortification was destroyed. Nevertheless, even with its small size, the wall gives archaeologists important information about Roman masonry techniques, especially because it is the only part of the Northern side of the wall that has been preserved. An interesting feature is the irregular use of red Roman tiles in between the layering of stone. This was used to ensure the wall remained level over the long stretch of defence.

The Londinium wall was built as one big project in the 2nd century CE. It was over 4 metres high, linking the different entry gates of the city, and people would

travel to the different gates via a parapet walkway. It is strange to think that the once-elevated defences are now buried deep below ground in a dark carpark, but the whole land level of London itself has increased by about 18 feet over the last 2,000 years. Who knows how much more of the 2-mile wall is still to be found in the underground basements, cellars, and carparks of London…

ANOTHER SECTION OF THE ROMAN WALL DEEP UNDERGROUND

There is one other section of the Roman wall that can be discovered only by venturing deep underground, but this one needs a tube ticket to see it. On the wall opposite the westbound platform of Tower Hill station is a small rectangular hole, enclosed by black stone. Peer through this gap (from the safety of the platform) and you will see the ancient bricks still standing behind the tunnel wall.

There is also a sign pinned to one of the pillars of the platform which explains that the legacy of the wall lives on in the names of the tube stations located where the old Roman gates were such as Moorgate and Aldgate.

08.

Tower Hill, EC3N 4DJ
Tower Hill or Moorgate tube

LONDON WALL

A Roman hunk

Like most great European cities, London is a palimpsest of generations of building. What we mostly see today is a very strongly built Victorian city, on top of dainty Georgian foundations that retain the medieval street pattern that was laid over the original Roman plan.

Ghosts of the Roman past litter the city, but require a certain amount of seeking out. The Temple of Mithras on Walbrook Street is one example. Battle Bridge in King's Cross is another – reputedly the site of the final battle between the Romans and Boudicca, who is buried, legend has it, under Platform 9 at King's Cross station.

However, the largest remains are those of the defensive wall built by the Romans after Boudicca sacked the city in 60 CE (the only time the city has been utterly wiped out), which remained largely intact for the next 1,000 years. London Wall is mostly built from stone shipped up the River Thames from Maidstone in Kent. Originally enclosing an area of about 1.3 km², in comparison to the monstrous 1,579 km² that Greater London has become, the wall stretched from Blackfriars in the west, via Ludgate, Moorgate and Aldgate to the Tower of London in the east.

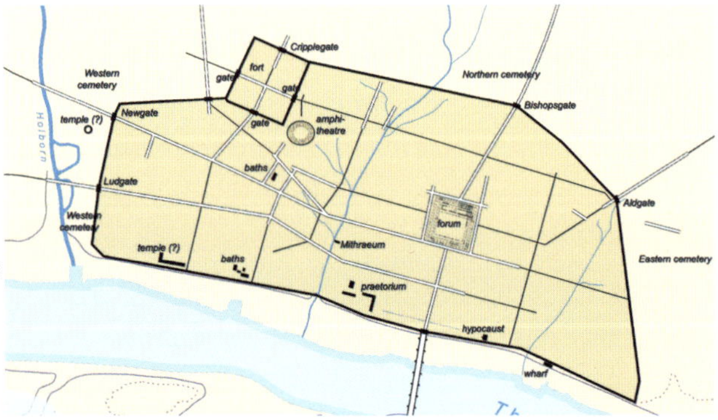

London Wall must have been an astonishing edifice in Roman times. It stood about five metres high, with a 2-metre-deep ditch in front of it, and was lined with a number of bastions. The best preserved of these is in the Barbican estate, next to the church of St Giles-without-Cripplegate – a fragment of old London entirely surrounded by an extremely modern landscape.

What remains of London Wall today is largely the core, as much of its facing and cut stone was carted off for other building after the Romans left Britain. The biggest intact section lines the street now known, imaginatively, as London Wall. Other chunks stand at Tower Hill and within the Museum of London, but a careful walk of the streets that would have formed the wall often turns up other bits and pieces.

The oddest location for a fragment of Roman London is on display in the basement of Nicholson and Griffins (www.nicholsonandgriffin.com), a hairdresser in Leadenhall Market. This is the base of an arch in what was the city's basilica, or civic centre. At over 150 metres, it was the same length as St Paul's, and the largest building north of the Alps in 150 CE. This suggests that London was not a colonial backwater of the Roman Empire.

09.

The London Centre, Guildhall, Aldermanbury EC2V 7HH
Bank, St Pauls or Liverpool Street tube

NEW LONDON ARCHITECTURE

A glimpse into London's future

In the ground floor galleries at New London Architecture (NLA), a think thank dedicated to the capital's built environment, is a monumental 1:2000 scale model of central London. 12.5 metres long and featuring some 170,000 buildings, it covers more than 85 square kilometres, from King's Cross in the north to Peckham in the south, and the Royal Docks in the east to Old Oak Common in the west.
Through interactive projections and illuminations, historic events, such as the Great Fire of London, and new developments, such as Crossrail, can be digitally animated across the surface of the model. Using touchscreens, visitors can call up key facts about the future projects and landmarks that will shape the capital.
With 263 skyscrapers in the pipeline, the model offers an unnerving glimpse into the future, as the land grab by property developers and overseas investors continues to swallow whole chunks of London.
Billing itself as 'a vital addition to the public debate about the future of London', the NLA hosts talks about the opportunities and challenges for urban regeneration, from waste management to affordable housing.
Architectural walking tours of 8 central London neighbourhoods – taking place on the second Saturday and last Wednesday of each month – reveal how the capital's streetscapes are changing.
There's an excellent architectural bookshop and reference library, as well as a cute little café populated by bespectacled architects clad in standard issue monochrome.

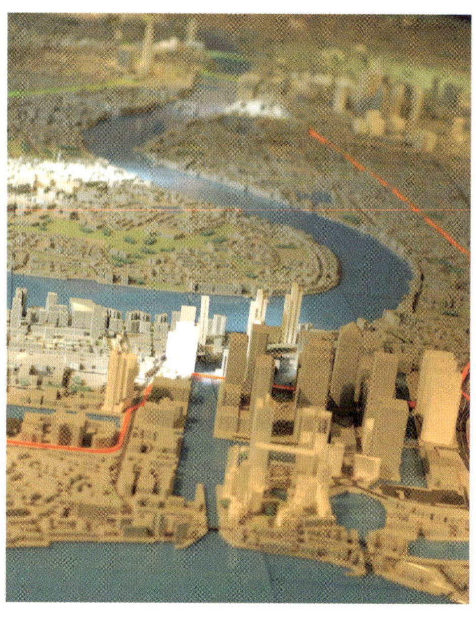

10.

40 Liverpool Street, EC2M 7QN
Liverpool Street tube/rail

THE MASONIC TEMPLE AT ANDAZ HOTEL

Occult lodgings

With its distinctive red brick façade, the former Great Eastern Hotel is an impressive Victorian landmark beside Liverpool Street station. Built for the Great Eastern Railway Company, the hotel was designed by Charles and Edward Barry, whose father (another Charles Barry) built the Houses of Parliament.

When it opened in 1884, the Great Eastern Hotel had its own tracks into the station for the delivery of provisions, including sea water for the hotel's salt-water baths. Despite this swanky heritage, the hotel gradually fell into disrepair until restaurateur Terence Conran snapped it up in the late 1990s and embarked on an extravagant makeover.

During the renovation, concealed behind a false wall, the builders were surprised to discover a wood-panelled antechamber leading to an intact Masonic temple. Decked in 12 types of Italian marble, with a blue and gold ceiling decorated with the signs of the zodiac and a mahogany throne at either end, this Gothic showstopper was built in 1912 for £50,000, the equivalent of around £4 million today. The Freemasons, who helped to build the Great Eastern Hotel, held clandestine meetings here for decades.

A second temple, decorated with Egyptian motifs with seating around a chequerboard floor, was discovered in the basement. Evidently not intimidated by the occult, Conran converted it into a gym.

Now owned by the Hyatt hotel group, the building has been rebranded as the Andaz.

To avoid tampering with the original architectural fittings, the Andaz is fitted with vacuum drainage like that used on planes. So when you flush the toilet, the waste is sucked upwards and disposed of through the hotel roof.

11.

St Ethelburga's Centre for Reconciliation and Peace, 78 Bishopsgate, EC2N 4AG
Liverpool Street or Bank tube

THE TENT

Peace camp

It's easy to walk past St Ethelburga's without noticing it. The slender church sits quietly amid the hubbub of Bishopsgate, with its high-rise offices and harried bankers. When it was founded around 1400, St Ethelburga's was the largest building on Bishopsgate: today, it's the smallest.

Behind the medieval façade is a surprisingly modern interior, empty apart from a simple wooden altar and a handful of artworks. Though it survived the Great Fire and the Blitz, the church collapsed after an IRA bomb blast nearby in 1993. Fragments of the original features were salvaged to create this new space. Though consecrated, it's no longer technically a church; there's no parish and no priest. It's now a Centre for Reconciliation and Peace, focusing on the role of faith in war and conflict resolution.

The derelict land behind the church has been transformed into a peace garden (also accessible via an alleyway off Bishopsgate). With its intricate mosaic tiling and tinkling fountain, it's like stepping into a Moroccan riad. The centrepiece is The Tent, a 16-sided structure with walls of woven goats' hair, modelled on traditional Bedouin tents. Tents are also associated with the nomadic origins of Judaism, Christianity and Islam – just the thing for a sacred space dedicated to inter-faith dialogue. Take off your shoes and step into a serene cocoon, carpeted with rugs woven in conflict regions and lined with low benches. The seven stained-glass windows contain messages of peace written in Chinese, Sanskrit, Arabic, Japanese, Hebrew, English and Inuit. Even the occasional siren cannot shatter the peace.

The Tent hosts devotional gatherings, meditation, storytelling and recitals. In the main building, you might stumble upon a Tibetan sand mandala, an Afro-Cuban concert or a discussion on civil disobedience. The unifying philosophy underlying all these events is that peace begins within.

St Ethelburga's has a long tradition as a progressive church. William Bedwell, rector from 1601 to 1632, was an Arabic scholar. In 1861, rector John Rodwell published the first reliable English translation of the Qur'an (still in print). And in the 1930s and 1940s, this was one of the few churches in London where divorced people could remarry.

12.

2 Henage Lane, EC3A 5DQ
Aldgate or Liverpool Street tube

BEVIS MARKS SYNAGOGUE

The oldest synagogue in England

Opened in 1701, Bevis Marks is the oldest synagogue in England. It was established by Spanish and Portuguese Sephardic Jews in response to a surge in congregation numbers at the small synagogue in Creechurch Lane, when Cromwell unofficially re-admitted Jews into England after their expulsion in 1290 by Edward I.

Cromwell never formally revoked the expulsion, but made it clear that the ban would not be enforced. The government hoped to profit from their connections with the mercantile centre of Amsterdam as England grew into a global trader. The ultra-Protestant Cromwell believed that the conversion of the Jews to Christianity was essential before Christ's return to reign on Earth. However, it wasn't until 1858 that English Jews received formal emancipation.

The synagogue is tucked away in a courtyard approached through a stone archway, and is largely unchanged since its construction three centuries ago. It is the only synagogue in Europe that has held regular services continuously for over 300 years. Above its doors is inscribed A.M. 5461, the Hebrew year in which it was opened. Its interior resembles a Wren church, although its décor, furnishing and layout are clearly influenced by the 1675 Portuguese Synagogue in Amsterdam. Embedded in the roof is a beam from a royal ship presented to the congregation by Queen Anne. The Ark (which holds the scrolls of the Pentateuch) at the east end reflects the late 17th-century taste for classical architecture, again in the manner of Wren. The synagogue also has a very good collection of Cromwell-era and Queen Anne furniture, which remain in regular use.

Aldgate was the 19th-century centre of London's Jewish community. There are still vestiges such as the dirt-cheap, 24-hour bagel shops at the top of Brick Lane, but mostly there are ghosts: Jewish schools, bath houses, and soup kitchens, now converted into gracious flats for City workers. Look out for the colourful mural commemorating the Jews of the East End, opposite the Brune Street Soup Kitchen. The arch on Wentworth Street is the only survivor of the Four Percent Industrial Dwellings Company, founded in 1885 by Sir Nathaniel Rothschild to clear the area's slums and provide decent housing for Jewish residents – albeit with a 4% profit for investors. Now one of London's largest mosques, the synagogue at 59 Brick Lane used to be so busy that classrooms were built on the roof – look up and you can still see them.

13.

The Tower Hotel, St Katharine's Dock, E1W 1LD
Tower Hill tube

THE QUEEN'S SILVER JUBILEE MONOLITH

The monolith that did not make it into Stanley Kubrick's film '2001: A Space Odyssey'

Decorating the brick wall of the Tower Hotel on Cloister Walk, hanging slightly above eyeline and overlooking St Katharine's Dock, is the world's largest acrylic block. Measuring 3.2 by 1.75 by 0.2 metres, the block weighs a hefty two tonnes and is made from clear plastic, although it now looks like a dirty shade of transparent. Carved into the middle is a royal crown emitting rays of light. It is impressive, striking, and entirely out of place.

What brought this chunk of plastic to St Katharine's Dock was its unsuccessful career in the film industry. It was created in 1968 by a local plastics firm, Stanley Plastics, to star as the iconic monolith in Stanley Kubrick's film '2001: A Space Odyssey.' For those not enthusiastic about watching 2 hours 25 minutes of masterful but painfully slow (for many) sci-fi, the mysterious monolith can be found in only four scenes. It crops up when there is a profound shift in evolution, such as in pre-historic African savannah at the moment when humans learn how to use tools, or in lunar space when astronauts are exploring the moon.

In stereotypical Kubrick style, the monolith was symbolic and perplexing.

Its role in the film was never fully explained, which meant that the deeper meaning of the prop has been discussed, argued over, and interpreted many times: it

© Leo Reynolds

remains a controversial and renowned icon of cinema history.

Unfortunately for the transparent block now decorating St Katharine's Dock, Kubrick decided at the last minute that it wasn't nearly ominous enough: it was fired and replaced by the opaque black basalt model you see in the film.

So, what to do with the largest block of acrylic ever to be fired from set? In the end, it was kept in storage for almost a decade.

It was only in 1970s that a local sculptor and pioneer in Perspex plastic art, Arthur Fleischmann, was commissioned to create something with it to celebrate the Queen's Silver Jubilee.

Working from a temporary studio in St Katharine's Dock, Fleischmann set about carving a shining crown into the block. The sculpture was unveiled by the Queen in a ceremony in 1977, and was placed in the middle of an open-air, circular colonnade called the 'coronarium'.

In 2000 this unusually shaped structure was turned into a shop (it is now a restaurant) and the jubilee block was hung on the side of the Tower Hotel.

Despite its failed attempts to break into the film business, at least here the block will always have an audience.

14.

Tower Bridge Road, SE1 2UP
Tower Hill tube

TOWER BRIDGE BASCULE CHAMBER

Underwater engineering

Tower Bridge may be a preposterous structure – a colossal piece of Victorian engineering that someone has tried to disguise as a Gothic castle – but it's undeniably an eye-catcher. The standard tour of the bridge is pretty good, especially since the installation of the thrilling/horrifying glass floors in the pedestrian walkways linking the tops of the towers. If you get your timing right, you can look straight down onto the bridge when it opens, its jaws widening below you like a giant mechanical shark. (Check the website for bridge opening times.)

But if you book a place on the Behind-the-Scenes Personal Guided Tour (that really is what it's called!), you can delve into the bowels of this monster. Like most of its contemporaries, Tower Bridge was massively over-engineered to avoid any possibility that this most easterly of London bridges should collapse.

The high point – or in fact, the low point – of the tour is to one of the bascule chambers beneath the bridge's twin towers. Bascule means seesaw: all 422 tons of counterbalance swing down into these giant, wedge-shaped spaces when the bridge is raised. There are hundreds of safety measures in place, but that weight still looms above your head when you stand at the bottom of the chamber staring up. Noise from the traffic overhead bounces around the space and you can hear clearly when a bus or truck rattles by. Accessed via steep, narrow stairs, most of the chamber is well below the surface of the river, on the other side of 20-foot-thick walls. Consequently, this is one of the few rat-free spaces anywhere along the Thames. There's nothing for rodents to survive on – a bonus for muriphobes.

The acoustics in these cavernous vaults are phenomenal, and they are occasionally used for classical and contemporary concerts during the Thames Festival. However, the difficulty of getting large numbers of people in and out means that events are restricted in scale and number – check out the Festival's website well in advance for pre-booking.

In its heyday, Tower Bridge employed an operating staff of 96; this is currently down to 12, including the six bridge 'drivers' who control the bascule chambers from the north-east cabin. The bridge opens around 1,000 times a year; river traffic takes priority – even the King has to wait.

15.

Tower Hill, EC3N 4AB
Tower Hill tube

TOWER SUBWAY

A lost passage under the Thames

When Italian writer Edmondo de Amicis visited London in 1883, he described a '... gigantic iron tube, which seems to undulate like a great intestine in the enormous belly of the river'. This river monster was, in fact, Tower Subway, built beneath the Thames in 1869 to shuttle passengers between the north and south banks. All that survives of this engineering feat is a small, circular brick tower beside the Tower of London ticket office. This is not actually the original entrance to the Subway – it was built by the London Hydraulic Power Company, when they took over the defunct tunnel in 1897. The other entrance on Vine Street, south of the Thames, has been demolished.

Unlike its predecessor, Marc Isambard Brunel's Thames Tunnel, which cost £60,000, two lives and took almost eighteen years to complete, Tower Subway was built in ten months for £16,000 by a 24-year-old named James Henry Greathead. The tunnel's innovative structure, clad in an iron tube, was the template for London's first underground train, the City & South London Railway, built in 1890.

A dozen passengers were shuttled across the Thames in an 'omnibus' that ran along a single-gauge track. After a series of mechanical mishaps, this service folded after just three months and the tunnel was converted into a gas-lit walkway. Charles Dickens Jr warned: '... it is not advisable for any but the very briefest of Her Majesty's lieges to attempt the passage in high-heeled boots, or with a hat to which he attaches any particular value.' Though damp and claustrophobic, this did not deter the 20,000 pedestrians who used the subway every week, paying a halfpenny each way.

When toll-free Tower Bridge opened in 1894, Tower Subway became redundant. It was sold to the London Hydraulic Power Company for a measly £3,000. The water pipes have since been replaced by TV cables.

HYDRAULIC POWER

16.

1 Sky Garden Walk, EC3M 8AF
Monument or Bank tube

SKY GARDEN

Beauty on the beast

London's skyline has exploded upwards in the last ten years as property developers have sought to capitalise on the insatiable demand for housing. The City of London took the fight to Canary Wharf by building more 'signature' skyscrapers. There are always more to come – 2008 mayoral candidate Boris Johnson promised the electorate that he wouldn't allow the building of Dubai-on-Thames, but then, you know, he kind of did. In 2016 alone, there were over 430 new tall buildings planned for the capital. Some of these are welcome, but many of them simply dwarf the place.

Among the most notorious of the new showpiece builds is 20 Fenchurch Street, known as the Walkie-Talkie because of its shape. Completed in spring 2014, it promptly won the 2015 Carbuncle Cup for the worst new building in the UK. The concave glass wall at the front directs sunlight downwards, and in 2013 the construction company had to pay the owner of a car parked in the street below whose bodywork was melted by the building. The bulbous behemoth looms menacingly over Eastcheap, an ogre of a building that makes passers-by feel like ants.

However, the beast has a beautiful secret. The developers have constructed a huge light- and air-filled atrium at the top of the tower, with a balcony and a 360° view of London. Unlike the Shard, which sits directly across the river, entry is free, although the limited number of spaces means that online booking well in advance is essential. There are a couple of bars, a brasserie and a restaurant placed between two rising terraces of plants: they include figs and other flowers, shrubs and ferns that flourish all year round. The whole thing is wrapped in glass, with excellent unobstructed views (unlike the Shard). The effect is as if a minor greenhouse from Kew Gardens had been dropped on top of a skyscraper.

A CHURCH FULL OF SHOES

At the foot of 20 Fenchurch Street is St Margaret Pattens, a minor Wren church with an odd name (Pattens wasn't the saint's surname). These wooden-soled overshoes, later soled with iron rings, allowed the wealthy to walk the streets of London without muddying their shoes. The sound supposedly made the streets seem as if they were filled with horses. The church has long been associated with The Worshipful Company of Pattenmakers, and there is a display of pattens in the vestibule.

17.

Lower Thames Street, EC3R 6DN
Monument tube

LONDON BRIDGE MODEL AT ST MAGNUS THE MARTYR

London's first bridge

St Magnus the Martyr, tucked away near the Monument, is a seldom-visited Wren church in the shadow of London Bridge. The road to the original bridge, pulled down in 1831, once ran through the churchyard. Inside the church is a 4-metre-long model of the original bridge in its medieval incarnation, complete with the houses and shops that once lined it. The model is beautifully made, and crowded with tiny figures, giving some idea of how chaotic it must have been. At its peak, there were 200 businesses on the bridge, as well as a church. Just 4 metres wide, it was the only river crossing in London for livestock, horses, wagons and pedestrians until Putney Bridge opened in 1729. Unsurprisingly, crossing the bridge could take up to an hour. All of the tiny figures are authentically dressed in medieval costumes, with one exception...

The model of London Bridge also includes the heads of traitors set on spikes above the southern gatehouse. These were dipped in tar to preserve them against the elements. Oliver Cromwell's head was on display for at least 20 years after he had been dug up, ceremonially hanged and then decapitated.

VESTIGES OF THE FIRST LONDON BRIDGE

By the end of the 18th century, the bridge was clearly no longer fit for purpose as the city expanded – not only was it too narrow, but it obstructed the growing river traffic. The first step was to clear the bridge of its buildings: they were pulled down between 1758 and 1762. Several fragments remain, however: the coat of arms on the front of the King's Arms, in Newcomen Street south of the river, was once fixed above the entrance to the south gate of London Bridge. The arms are dated 1760, above the vigorous Lion and Unicorn; the pub itself dates back to 1890. The bridge remained in use until its demolition, but the road was widened and both sides lined with stone cupolas to shelter pedestrians. Two of these are now in Victoria Park in Hackney; far closer is the one in the courtyard of the Counting House, in what was the original Guy's Hospital, but is now part of King's College London. Walk straight through the gates of Old Guy's House on St Thomas Street, then through the arches ahead of you, and the cupola is on the left. Sitting inside is a statue of the poet John Keats, who trained at the hospital as a surgeon-apothecary between 1815 and 1816 (see p.194).

18.

Fish St Hill, EC3R 8AH
Monument or Bank tube

ASCENT OF THE MONUMENT

Pillar of strength

This oddity is much seen, but rarely visited. A single Doric column of Portland stone, the Monument contains an internal staircase of 311 steps winding up to a viewing balcony. When it was built in 1677, this would have afforded long-distance views; after 300 years of continuous building, the views are less spectacular. Once visible for miles, today visitors almost stumble across the column – the effect is like discovering a sailing ship in a canyon.

Designed by London's greatest architect, Sir Christopher Wren, and Dr Robert Hooke to commemorate the Great Fire of London, the 61-metre Monument is the tallest freestanding stone column in the world. The height is supposedly equal to the distance between the column and the baker's house in Pudding Lane where the fire reputedly began. It is topped by a flaming copper urn that symbolizes the Great Fire, but looks more like a flaming pudding. Originally, the column was to be topped with a phoenix (embodying the motto of London: '*Resurgam*' – 'I am reborn'), then with a colossal statue of King Charles II. But the committee responsible opted for the gilt pudding instead.

The walk up inside the column is precipitous: a thin handrail is all that lies between you and oblivion. Many visitors are undone by the climb, but each receives a certificate after getting up the damn thing. The summit was a favourite place for staging suicides until the balcony was fenced in with a metal cage. This cage is strong enough to support vigorous gymnastics and pull-ups, a very effective way of terrifying your friends.

Look closely and you will see that the base of the column is wrapped with a finely executed relief by Caius Gabriel Cibber, depicting a personification of London grieving before a backdrop of flaming buildings. Peace and Prosperity hover in the clouds, promising renewal, and King Charles II is on the right, all dressed up. Cibber is most famous for two statues, 'Melancholy' and 'Raving Madness', made for the gates of the infamous mental hospital Bedlam, which can still be seen at the Museum of the Mind. His son, Colley Cibber, a famously bad poet and actor, was the chief target of Alexander Pope's satirical poem 'The Dunciad'.

19.

St Magnus the Martyr, Lower Thames Street, EC3R 6DN
Monument tube

TIMBER FROM A ROMAN WHARF

A 2,000-year-old piece of timber

The stone walls of London's Roman city, Londinium, are a fairly common sight; although erected two millennia ago as part of a large defensive fortress, they were built to last. But Londinium's wooden structures have long since rotted, disintegrated and disappeared. All except one.

Tucked behind the church of St Magnus the Martyr is a 2,000-year-old piece of timber thought to be a historic relic of the old river wharf that was built near the first Thames bridge. After the bridge had been constructed, new buildings, platforms and wharfs were set up along the river. This quay would have been the centre of trade for Londinium, welcoming merchants, traders and visitors from around the Roman Empire: a vast number of people would have gathered here to trade basic necessities, luxury goods and enslaved people.

This piece of wood was found on Fish Street Hill in 1931 and brought to the churchyard to be preserved. Experts have dated the segment to 65–75 CE; it's been maintained over so many centuries because of a lack of oxygen in the waterlogged area that prevented the wood from decomposing.

It might seem odd to shelter something so ancient outside, but the timber's cosy corner in the portico underneath the bell tower of St Magnus the Martyr protects it from the elements.

20.

111 Cannon Street, EC4N 5AR
Cannon Street tube

LONDON STONE

Rock of ages

London Stone is back home again. This hunk of oolitic limestone was on display at the Museum of London while construction work took place at its traditional home, but was returned to a new case outside 111 Cannon Street in October 2018. It was originally larger and stood on the south of the street, but seems to have been damaged by the Great Fire of 1666. In 1720 what was left of it was housed in a stone cupola. In 1742 this was moved across the street, and later built into the wall of the new Wren church of St Swithin. Following the church's destruction in the Blitz, London Stone was placed in the Guildhall, before its 1962 return to Cannon Street. But where's it from?

Like many venerated objects, nobody really knows what London Stone is. One story has it brought to London by the Trojan Brutus, son of Priam, who fought and killed a race of giants led by Gog and Magog (whose images are still carried in the Lord Mayor's Parade) and erected a temple to Artemis with this stone as its altar.

Or it may be a Roman road marker. Or a Saxon one. Although there are no written Roman references to the stone, it was an important landmark after the city's foundation by the Romans. For hundreds of years, it was recognised as the symbolic heart of the City of London, before which deals were made, oaths taken, laws passed and official proclamations made. In 1450, the rebel Jack Cade struck his sword against it to signify his seizure of sovereignty after his forces had entered London.

London Stone has always attracted mystical enthusiasts. One legend has it as part of some kind of Druidic altar. William Blake, London's seer poet, imagined the groaning of the Druids' sacrificial victims in his poem, 'Jerusalem The Emanation of the Giant Albion'. Some people believe it sits on a ley line linking St Paul's and the Tower of London, making it a psychic lodestone for London. The truth is probably more boring (it usually is) – but London Stone isn't saying.

THE LONDON STONE LEY LINE

London's most powerful ley line – an alignment of ancient sacred places – runs along Cannon Street, connecting the churches of St Martin, Ludgate, St Thomas, St Leonard Milkchurch and All Hallows Barking, near the Tower of London. The hub of all ley lines in London is thought to be Ludgate Circus, where it is believed that a megalithic stone circle like Stonehenge once stood.

© GrindtXX

21.

Royal Exchange, between Cornhill and Threadneedle Streets, EC3V 3DG
Bank tube

THE ROYAL EXCHANGE AMBULATORY PAINTINGS

A pictorial history of England

Sandwiched between the Bank of England and Mansion House, the Royal Exchange is a grand repository of the city's history. The current building, with its sweeping atrium and arcade of luxury shops, dates from 1844. The original Royal Exchange – twice destroyed by fire – was founded in 1566 'as a comely bourse for merchants to assemble upon' by Sir Thomas Gresham, a merchant who cannily offered to build London a stock exchange at his own expense, in return for a lifetime interest in its profits. The building doubled as an Elizabethan shopping mall. The apothecaries and wig makers have been replaced by the likes of Boodles and Hermès, but the courtyard bar still thrums with the energy of commerce.

The pinstriped powerbrokers lunching in the mezzanine restaurants lining the space seem oblivious to the 32 paintings hidden in the shadowy recesses of the ambulatory. The tables face the courtyard, rather than these patriotic interpretations of landmarks in English history. Lords and ladies, kings and queens, admirals, cardinals and ordinary Londoners are shown feasting and fighting, trading and signing treaties. There are also statues of Elizabeth I and Charles II tucked away in the corners, all of which underlines the financial and political might of the city.

Until the 1950s, these images were used to illustrate school history books, but today they are overlooked. Many precious works, commissioned from the likes of Edwin Austin Abbey, J. Seymour Lucas and Sir Frederic Leighton (see p. 150), are concealed behind the restaurant kitchens, doomed to be splattered with bacon fat.

Even though the paintings are poorly lit and the titles are barely legible, they are still an awesome sight.

SHEPHERD'S BUSH TO MARYLEBONE

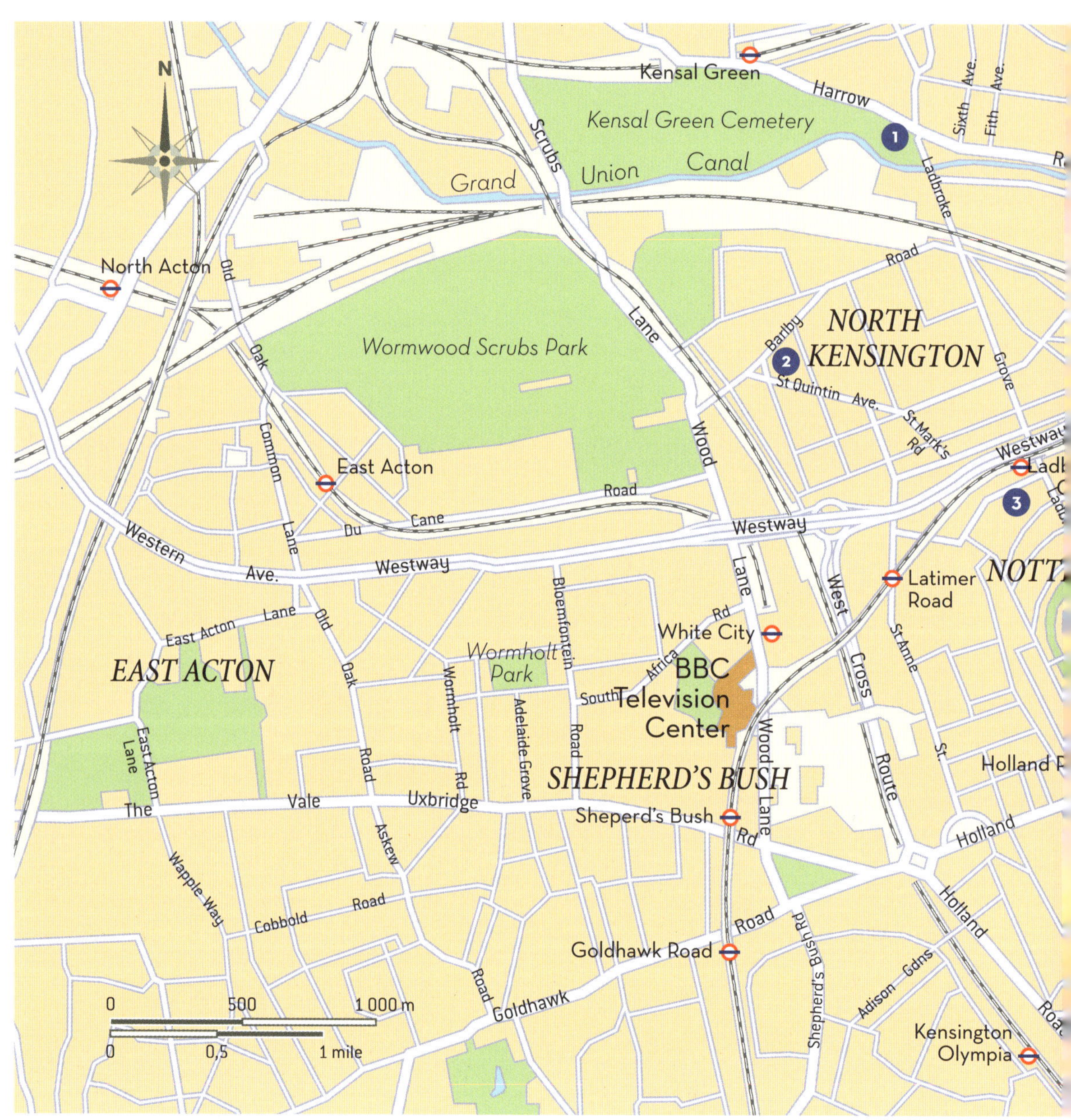

01. KENSAL GREEN CATACOMBS *p. 144*

02. WEST LONDON BOWLING CLUB *p. 146*

03. MUSEUM OF BRANDS *p. 148*

04. LEIGHTON HOUSE *p. 150*

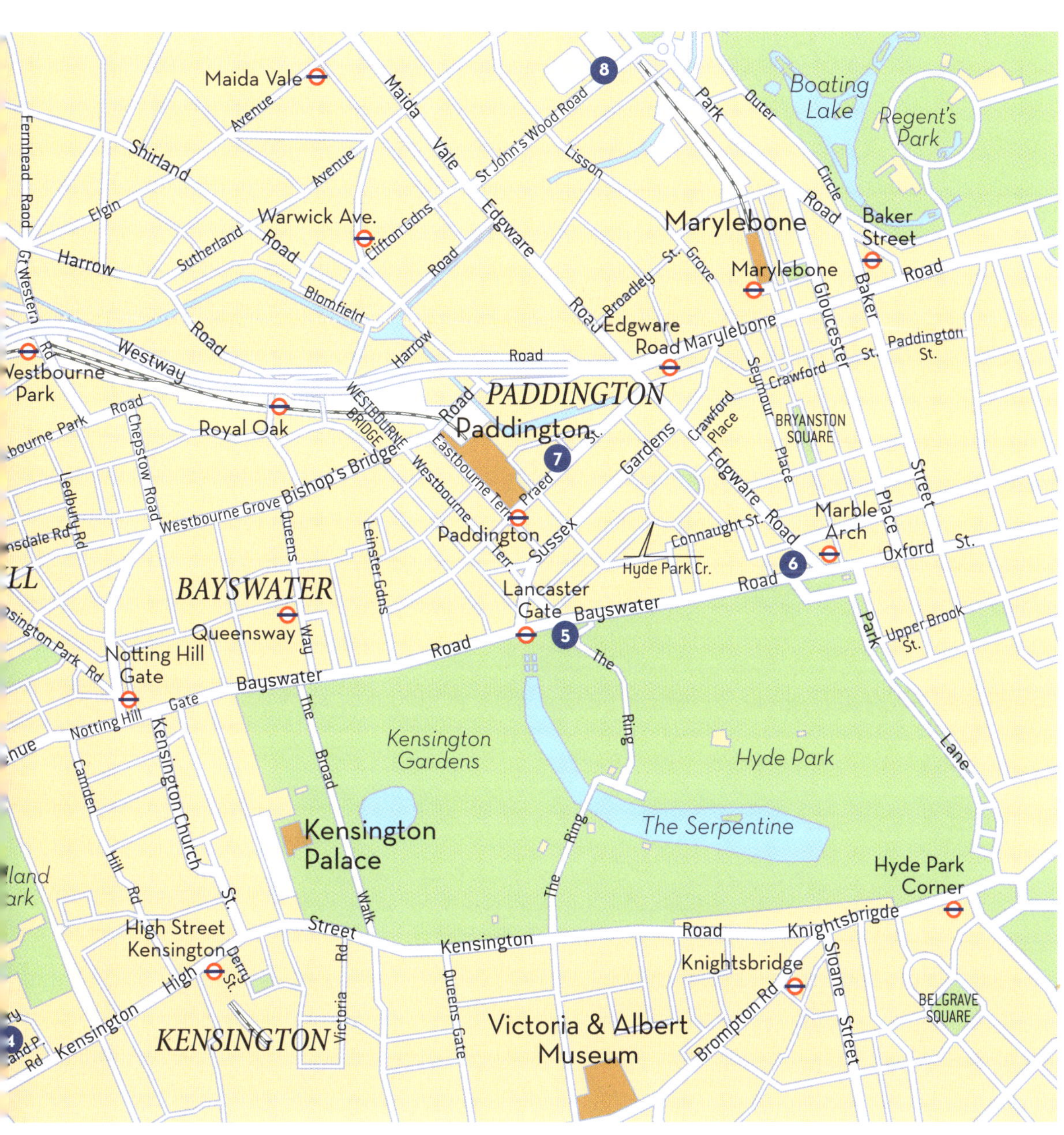

05. HYDE PARK PET CEMETERY *p. 152*

06. TYBURN CONVENT *p. 154*

07. ALEXANDER FLEMING LABORATORY MUSEUM *p. 156*

08. MARYLEBONE CRICKET CLUB MUSEUM *p. 158*

01.

Kensal Green Cemetery, Harrow Road, W10 4RA
Kensal Green tube/rail, Ladbroke Grove tube, Kensal Rise rail

KENSAL GREEN CATACOMBS

Dead and buried

The first of the 'Magnificent Seven' cemeteries that sprang up around London in the mid-19th century (see p. 282), Kensal Green is also the largest and most opulent. The Grand Union Canal runs along the cemetery's southern border, so you could even have a waterborne cortège.

Inspired by the Père Lachaise Cemetery in Paris, Kensal Green Cemetery became intensely fashionable after the Duke of Sussex was buried there in 1843. Other notable graves include those of Charles Blondin, who crossed Niagara Falls on a tightrope, pausing midway to cook and consume an omelette, and the fifth Duke of Portland. A paranoid recluse, the Duke built miles of gaslit tunnels, including a ballroom and billiards room, beneath his Nottinghamshire estate. He was so averse to human contact that his servants sent his roast chicken into his room on a model railway.

The Friends of Kensal Green, a conservation charity, offer regular tours of the cemetery, which include a descent into the extensive catacombs beneath the Anglican Chapel. The musty chapel contains the only working catafalque in the country, a hydraulic winch used to lower the coffins to the catacombs at a suitably funereal pace.

The catacombs are everything you might expect: damp, cold and dark. The brick avenues are lined with coffins stacked on shelves, sometimes behind glass, or iron grilles – mourners liked to be able to commune with the dead. Each coffin is triple shelled: a wooden casket inside a lead one, encased in an outer shell covered in scarlet velvet or metalwork. Most are covered in a powdery bloom where rot has set in. Some coffins are outlandishly huge, as if giants were buried within; others are instantly recognisable as children. Look out for a pair of glass domes containing *immortelles* – beautiful, lifelike flowers made from the finest porcelain and copper.

The catacombs are still functioning, and there is shelf space for sale if you're interested. Vacancies are marked with a grubby sign: 'Available'.

The catacombs are currently closed for essential conservation work. Until they reopen, visitors can peek into the smaller subterranean chambers beneath the Dissenters' Chapel.

WEST NORWOOD CATACOMBS

Founded in 1837, West Norwood was the world's first Gothic cemetery. Popular with millionaires, it contains the graves of Sir Henry Doulton, Baron de Reuter and Sir Henry Tate. The Greek Necropolis, where shipowners and merchants could flaunt their wealth even after death, contains the highest concentration of listed funerary monuments in Britain. The Friends of West Norwood Cemetery (www.fownc.org) organise monthly tours and occasional forays into the splendid Gothic catacombs.

02.

112A Highlever Road, W10 6PL
Latimer Road tube

WEST LONDON BOWLING CLUB

Roll up, roll up

I lived around the corner from this bowling green for a year before I realised it was there. Hidden at the end of a narrow alley wedged between two ordinary houses, the West London Bowling Club has been around since 1903. (It moved to the present site in 1920.)

Bordered by low-rise cottages, it was one of five 'backlands' created as communal recreation grounds for the residents of the St Quintin Estate, a leafy patch of West London that was a model of social and affordable housing long before former Prime Minister David Cameron and his ilk moved in. None of the other backlands has survived with its original use intact.

During the Second World War, while other backlands were turned into allotments, the club's members doggedly continued to bowl despite near misses by bombs and land mines. Men always wore whites. Their wives, who were not welcome on the green, had to make do with providing tea and cakes.

As one of the first female bowlers recalls: 'The year that man walked on the moon was the year that women were first allowed to walk on the green.' However, strict rules regarding the length of skirts were enforced for many years.

The popularity of bowling has waned since the club's mid-20th-century heyday. Membership dwindled, the green was unkempt and the prize-winning rose gardens became overgrown. The little clubhouse became a cheap drinking den, to the annoyance of the neighbours. Eventually the bowling club lost its licence and closed in 2013, but it has now been revived by a group of volunteers. Thanks to their efforts, the bowling club has been designated a 'local green space' that cannot be built over by developers.

Under new management, the bowling green has been relayed, a croquet lawn and petanque pitch installed, and the surrounding garden is gradually being spruced up.

The bowling season runs from mid-April to the end of September, with play from noon until one hour after sunset. Most afternoons, a few members show up for 'roll-ups' – casual games of barefoot bowls. There are occasional matches against other clubs, and experienced bowlers are usually on hand to coach beginners.

The bar is currently open on Fridays and Sundays in season, with film nights and social events year round. On a sunny summer evening, with the fragrance of freshly mowed grass and the thwack of croquet mallets hanging in the air, you could be back in the 1920s.

03.

111–117 Lancaster Road, Notting Hill, W11 1QT
Ladbroke Grove tube

MUSEUM OF BRANDS

A catalogue of consumerism

A visit to the Museum of Brands is like leafing through a picture book of Britain's social history over the last two centuries. Collector *par excellence* Robert Opie has assembled over half a million everyday objects, from Victoriana ('harness liquid' for carriages and 'wind pills' for sea sickness) through to royal memorabilia. Toys, cosmetics, candies and cleaning products – it's all here, artfully arranged by decade or theme. It's a time tunnel that takes you through the changing fashions and consuming passions of British society.

Once upon a time, banal products like shoe polish and cough syrup came in ornate jars and dainty decanters. Housekeepers stocked up on Vermin Killer ('Mice eat it readily and die on the spot!') and Desiccated Soup ('My dear, buy it!'). How times have changed from the days when 'Servants' Friend' stove polish was in vogue to the invention of the servants' friend: the first vacuum cleaner.

Opie's impressive hoard includes souvenirs from the Great Exhibition of 1851. There are wireless radios and wind-up gramophones, saucy postcards and cigarettes with 'guaranteed 22-carat gold tips'. From the art deco glamour of the 1930s, it's a jarring leap to the ration cards and trench football games of the Second World War, when people were exhorted to eat 'health salts' in lieu of fruit. The Win the War Cookery Book promises 'complete victory – if you eat less bread'. The 1950s bring a kitschy optimism, all colourful Formica, pin-ups in bikinis, and convertible cars for beach holidays. The '60s are summed up by the arrival of portable TVs and, of course, the Beatles. And what a decade the 1970s was: Planet of the Apes and platform shoes.

Graphic designers will delight in the Brand Hall, which revisits the evolution of classic British products like Cadbury's chocolate, Colman's mustard, and Kellogg's All-Bran (which has wisely changed its selling line from 'natural laxative' to 'high fibre'). The shop sells scrapbooks themed by decade, a useful source of inspiration for designers and illustrators.

The rather dreary café overlooks one of the museum's best features: a secret memorial garden that flowers all year round. Brimming with rambling roses and curious squirrels, the garden is the last vestige of The Lighthouse, a residential and day care centre for people living with HIV and AIDS, which occupied the premises until 2015. Many of the former patients' ashes are scattered in this lovely memorial garden.

QUAKER
Puffed Wheat
FREE SPACE AGE ZOOM-BALL
Kellogg's
SUGAR FROSTED FLAKES
Tony
MOBILE MODEL No. 4
THE LION
FRY'S
Hot CHOCOLATE
Cadbury's
BOURNVILLE COCOA
1 LB. NET.
Coffee Cup
French Coffee
NESCAFÉ
NESTLÉ'S
INSTANT COFFEE
LYONS
INSTANT
MAXWELL HOUSE Coffee
VITACUP
Brooke Bond
Choicest
Dividend
Sugar Puffs
QUICK
QUAKER OATS
Kellogg's
SUGAR
Ricicles
Grape-Nuts
BREAKFAST FOOD
Quofly
BISKS
Ambrosia
CREAMED RICE
(MILK PUDDING)
READY COOKED
You must try it, - it's delicious
WHITE'S
Flaked RICE
SAXA
Iodised table SALT
SIFTA TABLE SALT
STAG
COOKING SALT
Ah! BISTO
Brown & Polson
PATENT CORNFLOUR
KRAFT
SUPERFINE
MARGARINE
KRAFT
DAIRYLEA
CHEESE SPREAD
CREAM FOAM

CADBURY'S MILK
NUT MILK BAR
LYONS
FRY'S
5 BOYS
MILK CHOCOLATE
FRY'S FIVE BOYS MILK CHOCOLATE
FRY'S MILK CHOCOLATE
CARAM
GIANT SIZE
CRUNCHIE
CRUNCHIE
FRY'S
Walnut
CRISP WALNUT
Assorted
FOUR CRISP WAFER FINGERS
KitKat
3D

04.

12 Holland Park Road, W14 8LZ
High Street Kensington, Kensington Olympia or Holland Park tube

LEIGHTON HOUSE

Arabian maximalism

Many of the Victorian mansions around Holland Park were built by artists who gravitated to this urbane neighbourhood towards the end of the 19th century.
The 'Holland Park circle' included Lord Frederic Leighton (1830-1896), President of the Royal Academy, whose red brick show home looks fairly unassuming from the outside, apart from its dome.
Inside, Leighton House is designed to make a very big impression. Mary H. Krout, an American who visited in 1899, remarked: '…it was like a bit of Aladdin's palace, which some obliging genius might have set down in London and have forgotten.'

© Diego Delso

The entrance hall is clad in dazzling peacock blue tiles, while a real stuffed peacock guards the wooden staircase.
To the left is the Arab Hall, a floor-to-ceiling vision of rare Islamic tiles, inlaid mosaics, and Arabic inscriptions, with a black marble fountain as its centrepiece. The rest of the house is decked out in equally opulent style.
Flock wallpapers, oriental carpets, and ornate fireplaces create an orgy of patterns and textures, against which the pre-Raphaelite paintings by Leighton and his contemporaries look positively sedate.
By contrast, Leighton's bedroom is unexpectedly austere – perhaps he too needed a respite from so much oriental exotica.
Among Leighton's extensive art collection are works by Edward Burne-Jones, Albert Moore, and George Frederic Watts, who lived around the corner on Melbury Road. Leighton's own light-filled studio appears to be decorated with friezes filched from the Parthenon. This magnificent room was the setting for Leighton's annual music recitals; the tradition continues today with occasional chamber music and jazz concerts, with a smattering of socialites in attendance.

© Diego Delso

05.

Victoria Gate, Hyde Park, W2 2UH
Lancaster Gate, Marble Arch or Queensway tube

HYDE PARK PET CEMETERY

Bestial burial ground

Mad dogs and Englishmen have always been inseparable. The members of the Victorian upper crust were so obsessed with their pets that they buried them in special cemeteries. Barely visible behind the railings of Hyde Park, on the corner of Bayswater Road and Victoria Gate, hundreds of miniature, mildewed gravestones stand testament to this morbid tradition.

This particular pet cemetery was founded in 1880 by George, Duke of Cambridge, who had flouted royal convention by marrying an actress, Louisa Fairbrother. When his distraught wife's favourite dog, Prince, was run over, the Duke – who doubled as Chief Ranger of Hyde Park – asked the gate-keeper, Mr Windbridge, to give the poor creature a proper burial in the back garden of his lodge. By 1915, the graves in Mr Windbridge's garden were so tightly packed that the cemetery was closed. Over 300 animals are laid to rest here – dogs, cats, birds, and even a monkey. Drowned, poisoned, or run over, Flo, Carlo, and Yum Yum's miniature gravestones bear epitaphs that range from the touching to the maudlin. Quotes from the Bible and Shakespearean couplets are sprinkled among personal tributes: 'To the memory of my dear Emma – faithful and sole companion of my otherwise rootless and desolate life.' The unlikeliest epitaphs are to pooches named Smut and Scum. Some posh dogs even had bespoke coffins. One lady who buried her Pomeranian in a locked casket allegedly wore the keys around her neck until she went to her own grave.

This bestial necropolis received one last canine resident – also named Prince – in 1967, when the Royal Marines were granted special permission to bury their 11-year-old mascot in the southern corner. Today, the place George Orwell called 'perhaps the most horrible spectacle in Britain' can only be viewed by prior appointment.

CYP
OCTOBER

06.

8–12 Hyde Park Place, W2 2LJ
Marble Arch tube

TYBURN CONVENT

A cloistered existence

The highly desirable townhouses along Bayswater Road overlook Hyde Park, but the residents of Nos 8-12 can only enjoy these green vistas from a distance. Around 20 Benedictine nuns are cloistered here, maintaining a 24-hour vigil in the ground-floor chapel of Tyburn Convent. Though just moments from the bustle of Oxford Street, the nuns only venture out for medical emergencies. Food is delivered, but they don't do takeaways. The nuns spend most of their time in silence, broken by Mass, which is sung seven times a day, the ethereal music wafting through the chapel. Worshippers can hear, but cannot see the nuns: the altar is screened by a metal grille.

Tyburn Convent was founded in 1901 to commemorate the Roman Catholics hanged nearby on the Tyburn Tree gallows during the Reformation (1535 - 1681). The crypt contains a shrine to over 350 Catholic martyrs, including gruesome relics of their bones, hair, and bloodstained clothing. You can get a good look at these creepy appendages and keepsakes on one of the three daily tours of the shrine. Over the altar is a replica of the infamous Tyburn gallows, which stood just east of here, on what is now a traffic island at the junction of Bayswater Road and Edgware Road. A small, circular plaque in the paving stones marks the site where around 50,000 people were executed between 1196 and 1783. Hangings were so popular that execution days were declared public holidays. However, Mayfair's posh residents didn't like this barbaric spectator sport on their doorstep, and forced the authorities to move the gallows to Newgate (see p. 82) in 1783.

THE SMALLEST HOUSE IN LONDON

Now part of Tyburn Convent, the red brick 'house' at 10 Hyde Park Place is just over one metre wide. Apparently the ground floor consists entirely of a corridor, while the first floor contains nothing but a bathroom. Dating from 1805, it was probably erected to block a passageway leading to St George's graveyard – popular with body-snatchers at the time.

07.

St Mary's Hospital, Praed Street, W2 1NY
Paddington tube/rail, Edgware Road tube

ALEXANDER FLEMING LABORATORY MUSEUM

Mouldy microbes

A blue plaque outside St Mary's hospital alerts passers-by that Alexander Fleming (1881-1955) discovered penicillin in the second-storey room above it. Few visitors venture up to the tiny museum, accessible via a dingy entrance on Norfolk Place.

When Fleming was born, antibiotics did not exist. Minor infections often proved fatal and a quarter of all hospital patients died of gangrene after surgery. When Fleming enrolled as a medical student at St Mary's in 1900, he dreamed of becoming a surgeon; but – luckily for the rest of us – he was given a temporary position in the Inoculation Department, where he remained until his death.

The poky laboratory where Fleming worked between 1919 and 1933 (when it was converted into a bedroom for students of midwifery) has been painstakingly recreated. The wooden counter is cluttered with vials and test tubes containing mysterious fluids, tattered leather-bound medical tomes, a couple of antique microscopes and countless glass culture dishes. One day in 1922, Fleming was hunched over his bacteria cultures as usual, despite suffering from a nasty cold. A drop of snot landed on his Petri dish, which led to his discovery of the antiseptic properties of mucus, saliva and tears.

In September 1928, Fleming made another chance discovery that changed the course of medical history. When one of his cultures was contaminated with mould from a lab downstairs, Fleming hit on the healing properties of fungus – and effectively invented penicillin. Fleming's assistant, Stuart Craddock, ate some of this 'mould juice' to prove that it was not poisonous. Craddock claimed that it tasted like Stilton, prompting a flurry of sensational headlines about mouldy cheese being a miracle cure for disease.

'It couldn't have happened anywhere but this musty, dusty lab, as the mould would not have grown in a more hygienic environment,' says the museum's curator, Kevin Brown. The mouldy Petri dish in the museum is actually a replica – the original is in the British Library, along with several of Fleming's notebooks.

Alexander Fleming's grave in St Paul's Cathedral is decorated with the Scottish thistle and the fleur de lys, symbol of St Mary.

08.

Lord's Cricket Ground, St John's Wood Rd, NW8 8QN
St John's Wood, Warwick Avenue, or Marylebone tube

MARYLEBONE CRICKET CLUB MUSEUM

The world's oldest sporting museum

Although it has somehow acquired a reputation as a 'gentleman's game', at least to outsiders, early cricket fans were all chronic gamblers. In the 19th century, the wicket was prepared before a match by inviting sheep to graze on the grass. There is a waiting list of 18 years for membership of Marylebone Cricket Club (MCC). These are just a few of the surprising facts you'll learn if you 'take a tour of Lords', probably the world's most famous cricket ground. It's certainly one of the oldest, founded on a former duck pond in 1814 by a wine merchant named Thomas Lord.

The guided tour starts in the MCC Memorial Gallery, the world's first sporting museum. Among the signed bats, smelly boots, and old photographs spanning 400 years of cricket history, are oddities such as the stuffed sparrow that was 'bowled out' by Jehangir Khan in 1936.

The prized exhibit is a small Victorian perfume jar, containing 'The Ashes'. The term was coined after England lost to Australia on home soil for the first time on 29 August 1882. The next day, the Sporting Times published an ironic obituary to English cricket, concluding that: 'The body will be cremated and the ashes taken to Australia'. When the English team set off to tour Australia weeks later, Captain Ivo Bligh vowed to return home with The Ashes. After Bligh's team beat Australia, his future wife, Florence Morphy, gave him this miniature urn as a token of his victory. When Bligh died in 1927, he bequeathed The Ashes to the MCC where they have been on display ever since.

Visitors also have a rare opportunity to sneak around the 19th-century club rooms reserved for the 22,000 members of the MCC. On match days, at least 200 VIPs are crammed into the elegant Long Room, with its picture windows and paintings of celebrated cricketers. Players make their way to and from the field through the Long Room's double doors – either to rapturous ovation or deadly silence, depending on their performance. When the Queen cared to watch a match, she sitted in the Committee Room, where the worldwide laws of cricket are still thrashed out. But the best seats are undoubtedly in the Media Centre, a sleek white capsule that hovers 15 metres above the ground.

'THE WORST-BEHAVED CROWD OF THE SEASON'

The annual fixture between the pupils of Eton and Harrow has been played out since 1805. According to the tour guide, it's 'the worst-behaved crowd of the season.'

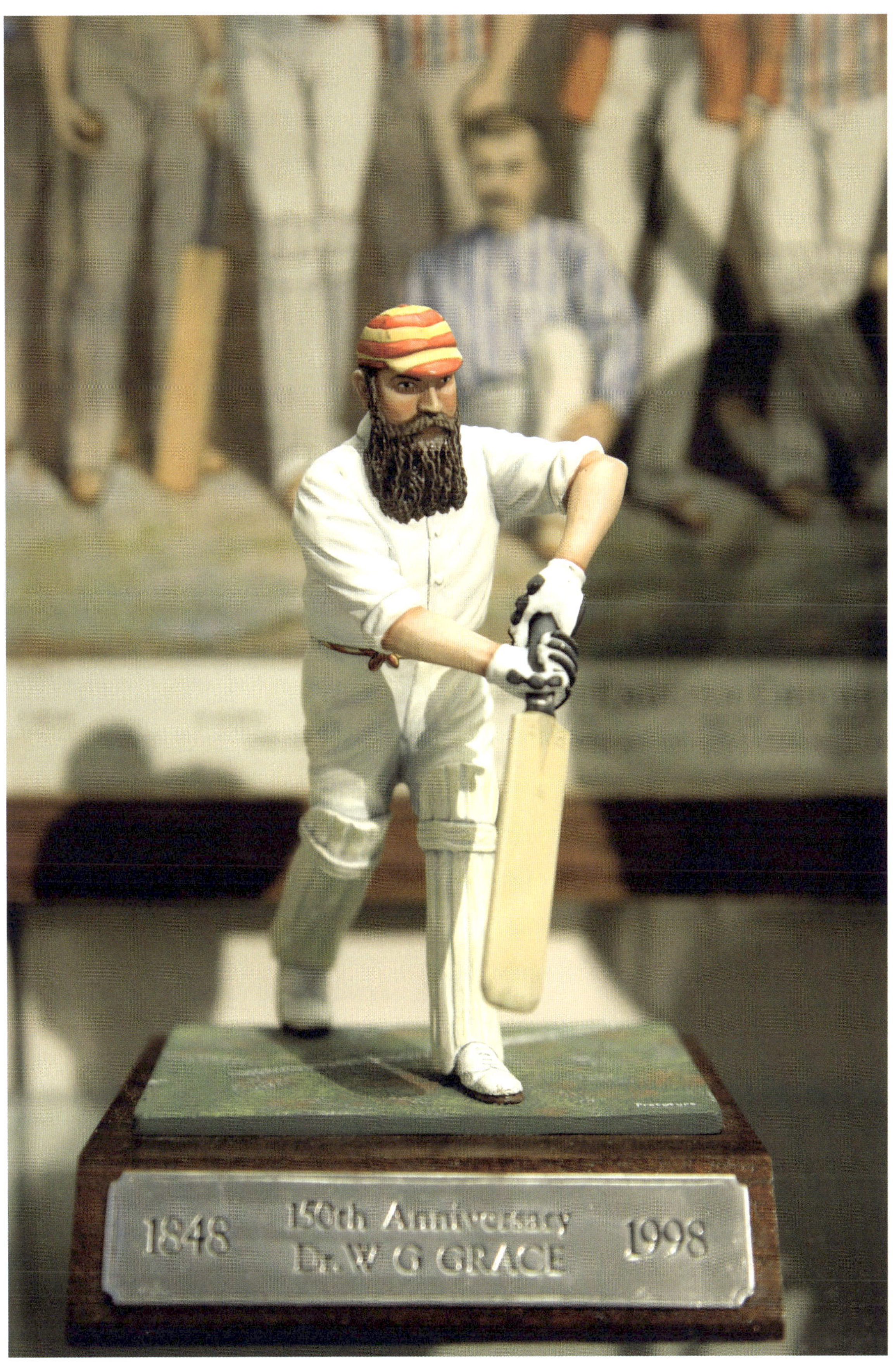
1848
150th Anniversary
Dr. W G GRACE
1998

HAMMERSMITH TO WESTMINSTER

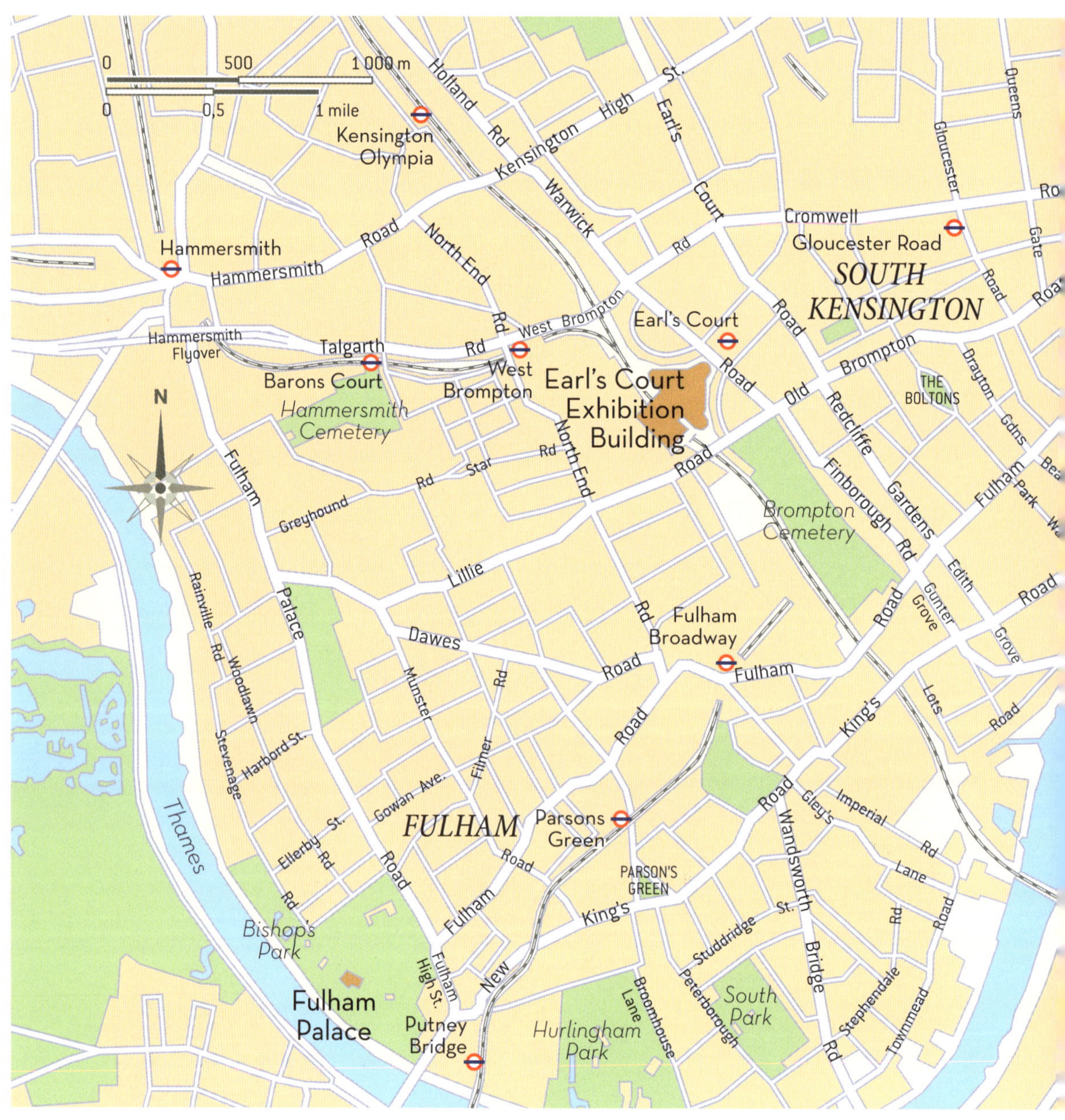

01. FETTER LANE MORAVIAN BURIAL GROUND *p. 162*

02. CHELSEA PHYSIC GARDEN *p. 164*

03. ROYAL HOSPITAL CHELSEA *p. 166*

04. THE LONDON SCOTTISH REGIMENTAL MUSEUM *p. 168*

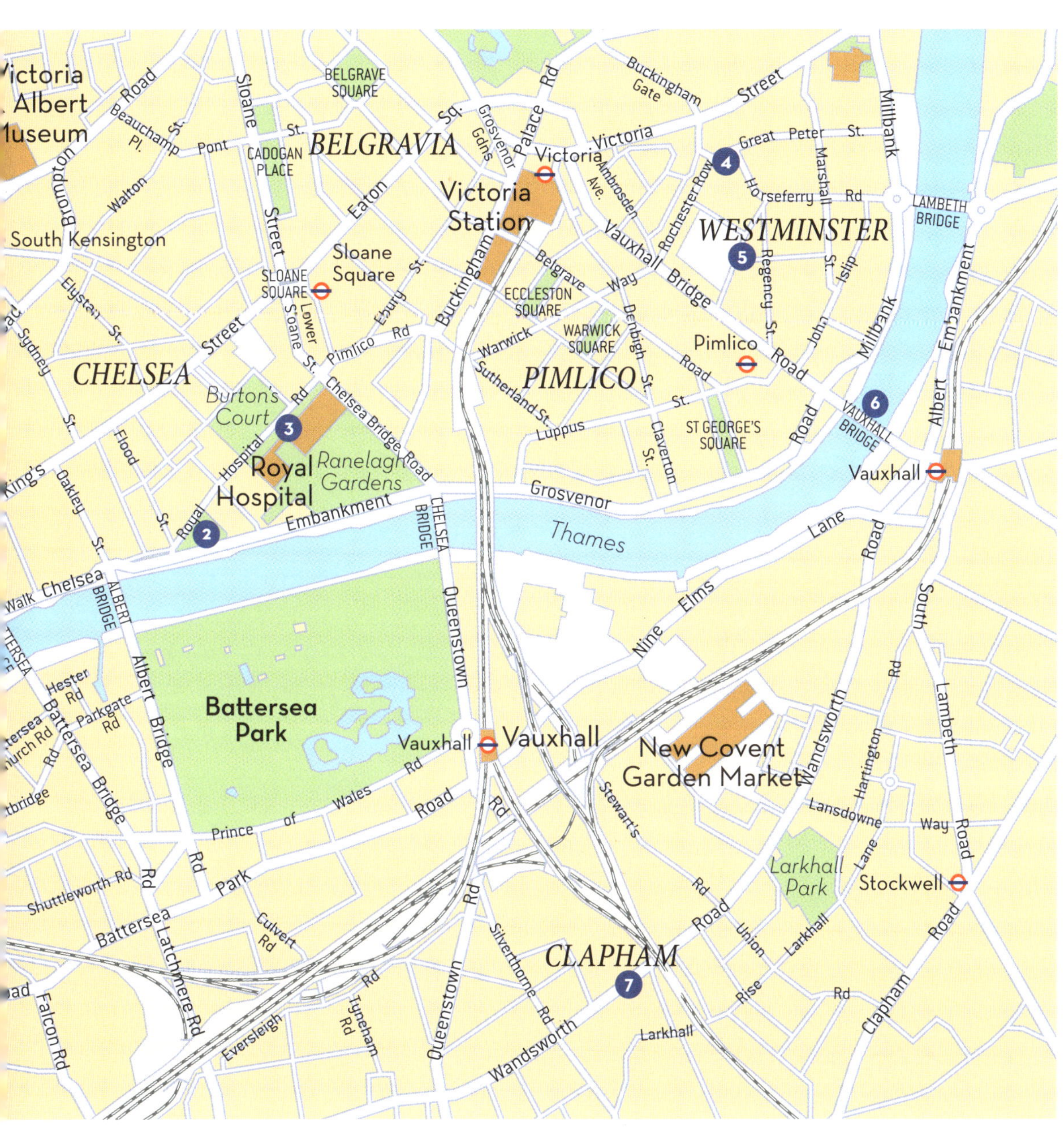

05. FIREPLACE *p. 170*

06. A MINIATURE ST PAUL'S CATHEDRAL *p. 172*

07. 575 WANDSWORTH ROAD *p. 174*

01.

381 King's Road, SW10 0LP
South Kensington, Fulham Broadway, or Sloane Square tube

FETTER LANE MORAVIAN BURIAL GROUND

Unmarked graves

World's End sounds like a good location for a graveyard. Hidden from the bouffant shoppers of King's Road by a high brick wall, this small cemetery adjoins the evangelical Moravian church. Established in 1742, the chapel looks like a country cottage transplanted into the heart of Chelsea. But the back garden is actually a burial ground. Known to the congregation as God's Acre, it contains a handful of 18th-century graves, marked only by flat, white stones. Traditionally, Moravians are buried separately in simple graves, men on one side and women on the other. The deceased are also sub-divided into those who are married and unmarried.

Originally from Bohemia and Moravia (now the Czech Republic), Moravians first came to Britain in the 1730s. The congregations created settlements with their own farms, businesses and schools. In 1750, their filthy rich leader, Count Zinzendorf, bought Lindsey House, a riverside mansion built by Henry VIII's ill-fated chancellor Thomas More, for £750. After a lavish renovation, the house became the international headquarters of the Moravian church and a resting place for missionaries. Its grounds stretched all the way from the waterfront to what is now the King's Road. Thomas More's former stables were converted into a church and the stable yard became the congregation's graveyard. However, the Moravian brethren never really took hold in London. After Zinzendorf's death in 1760, the property was divided into five townhouses and the church sold off most of the land, apart from this modest burial ground. Zinzendorf's son, Christian Renatus, is interred here, commemorated in a tablet on the south wall of the chapel.

Little remains of Thomas More's vast riverside estate, apart from the Tudor brick walls enclosing the Moravian burial ground. Roman Ambramovich and Mick Jagger have since occupied Lindsey House (now 100 Cheyne Walk). The Georgian mansion allegedly contains some religious murals painted by the Moravians. Owned by the National Trust, the gardens (subsequently re-designed by Edwin Lutyens) are accessible to visitors on Open House weekend.

A FELINE SLOANE RANGER

During the 1960s, the Moravian graveyard became the playground of Christian, a pet lion belonging to John Rendall, an Australian antiques dealer who bought the cub over the counter at Harrods. (Fittingly, Rendall's furniture shop on Kings Road was called Sophistocat.) The obliging vicar allowed Christian to play football in the safe confines of the parish grounds. Christian was later taken to Africa and rehabilitated into the wild.

02.

66 Royal Hospital Road, SW3 4HS
Sloane Square tube

CHELSEA PHYSIC GARDEN

Bankside botanicals

Horticulturalists and herbalists will delight in this enchanting walled garden containing around 5000 plant species from all over the world. The collection was founded in 1673 by the Society of Apothecaries to study the medicinal properties of plants. In 1712, Dr Hans Sloane, a wealthy physician, purchased the entire Manor of Chelsea. Ten years later, he leased some four acres of land to the apothecaries for £5 a year in perpetuity – a bargain even back then. The deed of covenant is on display, stating the garden's purpose, that 'apprentices and others may the better distinguish good and usefull plants from those that bear resemblance to them and yet are hurtfull.'

The location on the banks of the Thames created a warmer microclimate so that exotic plants could survive the biting British winter. Tropical plants are still cultivated in fetid greenhouses. The apothecaries' botanical experiments were influential in developing the American cotton industry and the tea trade in India. Given the 21st-century trend for natural medicine, the Garden of World Medicine and Pharmaceutical Garden were way ahead of their time. Look out for the bizarre pond rock garden, partially built with Icelandic lava and stones from the Tower of London. The café is also notable for its home-made cakes and lavender scones.

DR HANS SLOANE: INVENTOR OF MILK CHOCOLATE

As well as giving his name to Sloane Square, Dr Hans Sloane invented milk chocolate. After discovering locals drinking cocoa mixed with water in Jamaica, Sloane improved on the recipe by mixing it with milk. Back in England, his formula was sold as medicine until the Cadbury brothers cottoned on and began selling tins of Sloane's drinking chocolate.

© Elisa.rolle

03.

Royal Hospital Road, Chelsea SW3 4SR
Sloane Square tube

ROYAL HOSPITAL CHELSEA

Retirement home designed by Christopher Wren

Renting a small flat on Chelsea's Royal Hospital Road would set you back a small fortune. For the price of their monthly pension, the lucky 300-odd army veterans who live at the Royal Hospital Chelsea get to live in glorious digs designed by Christopher Wren, enjoy three meals a day served in an oak-panelled Great Hall lined with royal portraits, and have access to a clubhouse, library, bowling green, croquet lawn, billiard rooms, and 66 acres of gardens beside the Thames. They also get to wear snazzy uniforms – scarlet jackets and tricorne hats for special occasions, smart navy blazers and 'shako' caps for everyday wear.

King Charles II founded the baroque, redbrick Royal Hospital in 1682 as a refuge for 'the succour and relief of veterans broken by age and war'. Back in the 17th century, when recruits joined the army at the age of 11 or 12, only one in ten pensioners were literate. These days, the charming old boys are happy to show visitors around the small museum, which tells the history of this miraculous time warp through paintings, historical artefacts, and over 2,000 medals. There's even a model wooden berth, snug as a ship's cabin. Nine foot square, with no windows, these cubicles originally had no lights at all, let alone plugs for modern appliances.

Since 2015, the Chelsea pensioners' lodgings have been upgraded to include a private study and wet room. Women were welcomed for the first time in 300 years after en-suite bathrooms were installed. The Royal Hospital's residential halls are laid out around three immaculate quadrangles.

At 10:30 on Sunday mornings, from April to November, pensioners parade through Figure Court in their ceremonial finery. Only about a dozen have the energy or inclination these days. Listen carefully, and you might hear the master of ceremonies mumbling: 'Shuffle about, boys!' An infirmary was built some years ago. The only drawback is that rooms overlook their last posting – the cemetery. Chelsea pensioners must be over 65, 'of good military character', and have no dependents. When a pensioner applies for admission, they are invited to stay for four days to see whether the Royal Hospital suits them. Who would turn down the chance to live out their days in such magnificent surroundings?

04.

95 Horseferry Road, SW1P 2DX
Pimlico or St James's Park tube

THE LONDON SCOTTISH REGIMENTAL MUSEUM

From kilts to camouflage

Behind the sombre façade of this Territorial Army headquarters on Horseferry Road is a soaring drill hall, whose red and blue balconies are decorated with memorabilia from the London Scottish Regiment's colourful history.

A volunteer corps set up by a group of influential Scots in London in 1859, its distinguished members have included Sir Alexander Fleming, travel writer Eric Newby, and movie star Basil Rathbone.

Access is by appointment, which means that visitors get an exhaustive tour from the zealous archivist – though he may reprimand you if your military history is sketchy. Some of the army acronyms might be rather arcane for the non-expert, but only the coldest of heart will be unmoved by the memorials to the hundreds of untrained soldiers who served and died in the South African War (1900–02) and the Great Wars.

Around the upper floor balconies are all manner of medals, machine guns, bagpipes, uniforms, and photographs of 'old soldiers' going into battle in kilts and spats. There is even a scrap of Lieutenant-Colonel Lord Elcho's grey overcoat, which inspired him to invent the first form of camouflage. Fed up with soldiers from different clans bickering about tartans, Elcho decreed that the regiment should wear Hodden Grey, a coarse cloth typically worn in Scotland. This canny move also made the troops less of a target.

On Tuesday evenings, between 7pm and 9pm, the magnificent hall is used for drill practice, which must be a stirring sight.

HEAD QUARTERS
LONDON SCOTTISH RIFLE VOLUNTEERS

05.

109 Vincent STreet, SW1P 4BS
Pimlico tube

FIREPLACE

A domestic fireplace in the middle of a street

Built into the brick wall that stands at the corner of the gate leading to Dean Abbott House, at the point where Hide Place meets Vincent Street, is a strange-looking hole. Although partly covered by vines, you can still make out the shape and features of an old domestic fireplace, now attached to no chimney and no house.

A survivor from the war, the fireplace once belonged to a traditional Victorian terraced house, part of a row of houses that ran along Vincent Street. During the Second World War, these homes were hit by high-explosive bombs dropped from the air by the German air force during the Blitz. Houses all over the city were completely destroyed (around 1.1 million homes were hit according to historians) and Vincent Street was no exception. This area was under almost continuous fire between 1940 and 1941, probably because the factories there were prime targets – bombing factories was a key method used by the Germans to disrupt the war effort.

The Vincent Street fireplace has not only survived aerial attacks remarkably intact but also made it through 80 years of reconstruction and development. It is a very well-preserved fireplace: you can even see the metal grate at the back of the firebox. Many parts of Westminster stayed in their unhappy war-torn state for decades after the war. It was only in the 1980s that Vincent Street and the surrounding area was cleaned up and used for sheltered housing. The rubble was removed and new houses were built … but the fireplace stayed right where it was.

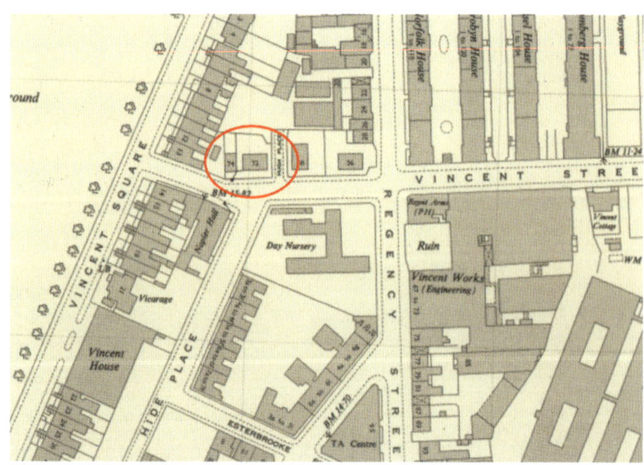

06.

Vauxhall Bridge, SW1V 3JN
Vauxhall tube

A MINIATURE ST PAUL'S CATHEDRAL

Britain's forgotten smallest cathedral

Peer over the south side of Vauxhall Bridge and you'll just about be able to see a miniature version of one of the capital's most iconic buildings. It has been called Britain's smallest cathedral and is a precisely scaled-down version of Sir Christopher Wren's 17th-century masterpiece, St Paul's Cathedral, located almost 5 km away. The model is held by a figure of a woman, the physical symbol of architecture, one of eight huge bronze statues that decorate the sides of Vauxhall Bridge.

When the New Vauxhall Bridge opened in 1906, the London City Council was worried that it wasn't attractive or interesting enough. The council's official architect, William Riley, suggested that allegorical statues could be placed along the sides, adding some interest and prestige to the bridge when seen by boats coming in and out of the city. The council supported the idea and two members of the New Sculpture movement (which emphasised naturalistic poses and spiritual subjects), Alfred Drury and Frederick Pomeroy, were hired as sculptors. Each was tasked with creating four colossal figures weighing around 2 tonnes that could be mounted to look out over the Thames.

All the statues along the side of Vauxhall Bridge are of women holding objects that represent some of the key foundations of London's life and soul. Drury created the figures facing downriver: the Fine Arts (holding a palette and a sculpted figure), Science (an orb), Education (two children) and Local Government (a book). Pomeroy took the ones facing upriver: Architecture (St Paul's Cathedral), Agriculture (a sheaf of wheat), Engineering (a steam engine, mallet and anvil) and Pottery (an amphora).

When they were first installed, the statues were much discussed in the national press, particularly because Vauxhall Bridge was the only bridge in Britain to have sculptures. However, people worried that because the figures were placed below eye-level, pedestrians wouldn't be able to appreciate the high-quality artwork. This was a legitimate concern.

Although at night these figures are lit up from above, creating a dramatic view when seen from the water, the eight women are hardly ever noticed from above. Over the years this neglect has worsened and the statues, as well as the country's smallest cathedral, have been almost forgotten by the millions of commuters walking, cycling or driving over the bridge.

07.

575 Wandsworth Road, SW8 3JD
London Overground/rail to Wandsworth Road

575 WANDSWORTH ROAD

Dreamy DIY

First things first. If you want to visit this singular house, book well in advance – ideally, months in advance. Visitors are strictly limited to 54 a week, with tours in groups of six people at a time. Since opening its doors to the public in 2013, the house of Khadambi Asalache, bequeathed to the National Trust, has attracted more visitors than it can accommodate.

From the outside, this unassuming house doesn't look like much. When the exiled Kenyan poet, novelist and philosopher of mathematics Khadambi Asalache bought it in 1981, the small, terraced house was in a bad way. Asalache, who trained as an architect but worked at the Treasury, fixed pine floorboards to the persistent damp patches on the walls and floors. He went on to cover almost every wall, ceiling and door in the house with delicate fretwork that he hand-carved with a plasterboard knife from pine doors and floorboards scavenged from skips. This pragmatic approach to his art characterises the whole project, and the National Trust has been careful to maintain it, retaining the Polyfilla used on the ceilings and a taped-up broken windowpane in the sitting room.

Asalache carved out this private sanctuary compulsively for the rest of his life. (He only once employed a carpenter, but dismissed his work as sub-standard.) Delicate ballerinas, angels, giraffes and birds dance over every surface. The astonishing fretwork was inspired by a mixture of the Moorish art of Andalusia, carved doors in Asalache's native Lamu, panelled interiors in Damascus, and the wooden mansions along the banks of the Bosporus in Istanbul. During conservation, over 2,000 pieces of woodwork were catalogued. The woodwork is juxtaposed with the painted decoration of the walls, doors and floors, hand-carved furniture and carefully arranged collections, including pressed-glass inkwells, postcards, and the poet's collection of pink and copper 19th-century English pottery.

The amount of stuff crammed into the house ought to be overwhelming, but the effect is quietly soothing. As the director of the Sir John Soane's Museum has said, it is 'an extremely serious and carefully worked-out exercise in *horror vacui* (fear of the void)' – and it works. In fact, 575 Wandsworth Road shares the compulsive nature of its interior with the Soane Museum. There is a huge amount to see in such a small space. The best bit? Possibly the main bedroom, with its shutters decorated with the initials of Khadambi and his partner Susie Thomson, and the kennel carved for Thomson's Tibetan spaniel next to the bed.

National Theatre
Tate Modern
City Hall
London Bridge
Waterloo
SOUTHWARK
THE BOROUGH
LAMBETH
Imperial War Museum
Elephant and Castle
VAUXHALL
KENNINGTON
WALWORTH
Burgess Park
Kennington Park
KENNINGTON OVAL
CAMBERWELL
Myatts Fields
Ruskin Park
BRIXTON
Thames
0
500
1 000 m
0
0,5
1 mile

SOUTH BANK TO BRIXTON

01.

Roupell Street, SE1 8TB
Southwark tube or Waterloo East rail

ROUPELL STREET CONSERVATION AREA

The historic enclave

The station of London Waterloo East cuts through time. On one side of the station is a place that defines modern London living. It is an area overflowing with trendy cafes, supermarket chains and cocktail bars. On the other side of the station, however, is a street that is eternally frozen in the 1820s. This is Roupell Street, a stretch of residential road that has been saved from development or progress and looks exactly how it did in the 19th century – although now with perhaps a few 21st-century cars parked outside.

Before development, this land was mostly taken up by marshland, sandbanks and tributaries of the river Neckinger (a subterranean river than occasionally pops up around Southwark). But calls for cheap affordable housing were increasing. The first houses on Roupell Street were built in the 1820s by a metal merchant called John Palmer Roupell. By the end of the decade there were thirty houses that were almost complete. Then suddenly disaster struck. The builders, working quickly to get the houses finished, accidentally knocked over a pot of boiling liquid and set the houses on fire. The blaze didn't spread far and was soon put out, but it set back the project a few years and added a large sum to the cost of building. The hastily added fire insurance plaques from this time can still be found on the walls of the houses as a reminder of this moment in the street's history.

After another five years, the houses were finally ready to be rented out to skilled local workers. They haven't changed much since then: Roupell Street escaped the encroachment of the railways as they expanded across the country, as well as the destructive bombing during the blitz that destroyed so many other beautiful London streets. It was very lucky and, two hundred years later, snug corner pubs, traditional lamp posts, and vintage cars continue to add to the historical magic of the place. In 1976 the street was given conservation status by Lambeth Council to save all the properties being sold individually to different owners, and many of the houses themselves were listed for historic conservation at this time.

Despite being a hidden gem, the street has appeared in some high-profile media productions. 'Call the Midwife', 'Legend', and 'Doctor Who' have all featured scenes filmed along Roupell Street's charming façade.

ROUPELL
STREET SE1
WINDMILL
WALK

02.

St Thomas' Hospital
2 Lambeth Palace Road, SE1 7EP
Westminster or Lambeth North tube, Waterloo tube/rail

FLORENCE NIGHTINGALE MUSEUM

To the bedside manner born

A hospital car park isn't the most obvious location for a museum – even one with a medical theme. But that's where you'll find this homage to Florence Nightingale, the genteel rebel who invented the nursing profession.

'There is nothing like the tyranny of a good English family,' Florence once sniped. She came from wealthy but liberal stock: her grandfather campaigned to abolish slavery and her father taught both his daughters mathematics, philosophy and science, then considered strictly male pursuits. The Nightingales also loved to travel; their honeymoon lasted so long that they produced two daughters (in Naples and Florence) before they returned home.

Devout and scholarly, Florence was not expected to do anything much apart from marry and procreate. She was certainly not supposed to work, but her ambition was to become a nurse. Her parents were aghast; in the Victorian age, nurses were known for being devious, dishonest and drunken. Hospitals were filthy, dangerous places exclusively for the poor; the rich were treated in the privacy of their own homes.

Undeterred, Florence set off for the Crimean War at the age of 34, with no formal training and very little experience. She spent two years nursing injured soldiers at the Scutari military hospital in Turkey, where she had to contend with rats, lice, cockroaches and an absence of sewage. In Britain, penny papers popularised the image of the 'lady with the lamp' patrolling the wards.

Although Florence hated the 'buzz fuzz' of celebrity, her famous lantern is the prize exhibit at the Florence Nightingale Museum. Dimly lit and curiously curated, with circular display cases covered in fake grass or wrapped in bandages, the small museum is packed with fascinating exhibits, from Florence's hand-written ledgers and primitive medical instruments to pamphlets with titles like 'How People May Live and not Die in India'. The most bizarre item is Athena, Florence's stuffed pet owl, whom she rescued on a visit to the Parthenon. Athena always perched on Florence's shoulder or in her pocket, with a specially designed pouch to catch her droppings. When the bad-tempered owl died, Florence wrote: 'Poor little beastie, it was odd how much I loved you.'

After contracting 'Crimean fever', Florence suffered ill health until her death aged 90. Unable to continue nursing, she devoted herself to health reform, founding the first training school for nurses at St Thomas' Hospital, campaigning to improve hospital ventilation, sanitation and nutrition, and championing the cause of midwives. Florence never married. She rejected several suitors, including one Richard Monckton Milnes, a devotee of the Marquis de Sade with an extensive collection of erotica.

03.

Lambeth Palace Road, SE1 7LB
Westminster or Lambeth North tube

GARDEN MUSEUM

Admire a rare cucumber straightener

The Garden Museum, which reopened in 2017 after undergoing redevelopment, may be one of London's best connected museums. Created from the former church of St Mary-at-Lambeth, it sits in the shadow of Lambeth Palace, residence of the Archbishop of Canterbury since 1200 and across the river from Westminster. This closeness to the heart of the UK establishment is probably about right for it – gardening is a British obsession from top to bottom, and this is the first gardening museum in the world.

The museum was founded by John and Rosemary Nicholson, after tracing the tomb of the 17th-century royal gardeners John Tradescant the Elder and Younger to this churchyard. Both men travelled widely and introduced a huge variety of trees and plants to British gardens.

The redevelopment, which included an expanded mezzanine inside the church, has allowed more of the vast collection to go on display. Jewels of this inlcude a cucumber straightener and a collection of garden gnomes. The café, one of the best in any London museum, also got an overhaul.

The museum's beautiful, if small, grounds include a 17th-century-style knot garden. These geometric and highly formal compositions were typically lined with clipped low hedges. The churchyard contains some noteworthy graves, including the tyrannical Captain 'Breadfruit' Bligh of the Mutiny on The Bounty.

A plaque to the left of the church's front door commemorates Brian Turbeville, Gent., who bequeathed £100 to St Mary-at-Lambeth for the apprenticeship of two poor boys each year. The museum also hosts occasional concerts and lectures. Education is set to become a more prominent part of the museum's brief – watch out for talks and evening symposia.

LAMBETH PALACE

Lambeth Palace contains some of the few surviving Tudor buildings in the capital, notably the red brick gatehouse built in 1495, as well as the Lollard's Tower, visible from the outside. Although the Lambeth Palace garden was split in two to create Archbishop's Park in 1901, it is still the second-largest garden in London after that of Buckingham Palace. Lambeth Palace is open to the public for the annual Lambeth Parish Fete and on Open House weekends. Check the Archbishop's website (archbishopofcanterbury.org/about/about-lambeth-palace) for details.

04.

Bonnington Square, SW8 1TE
Vauxhall tube

BONNINGTON SQUARE PLEASURE GARDEN

A secret urban jungle

A few minutes away from the concrete cityscape of Vauxhall, Bonnington Square consists of houses that have been taken over by vines, shrubs and flowers. Almost every building has some sort of wild or cultivated plant display to admire. In the corner of this wonderfully overgrown square is a tiny public park which has been designed to create a friendly jungle oasis in the middle of the city: this is Bonnington Square Pleasure Garden.

The pleasure garden is eccentric to say the least. To enter the park, you must first walk under a giant sculpture of a human hand – a sign of the garden's community spirit and a welcoming gesture for newcomers. Inside, the path weaves around the different sections of this small garden: the swing set, the secluded bench underneath drooping trees, the stone seats set in flowerbeds and the intriguing giant wheel (saved from an 1860s marble factory), all framed by native and tropical species.

In the 1980s Bonnington Square was scrap land still recovering from being bombed in the Second World War: the garden space was a derelict playground and the houses were mostly occupied by squatters. Eventually, however, the people living in the area managed to get together the resources to buy some of the houses from the council and they set up a co-operative organisation to create a sense of community spirit. Shops and cafes were supported communally and Bonnington was recognised as one of the UK's most successful experiments in 'social living'. The Bonnington Square inhabitants had the idea for a community garden in the mid 1990s. A builder had recently requested permission from the council to store equipment on the unused waste ground and the locals were quick to stake their claim to the space. The Bonnington Square Garden Association was formed and, after receiving funding, set about creating a pleasure garden for the locals. Now it is a vibrant space, expertly cultivated and still contributing to the friendly community atmosphere of Bonnington.

The name Bonnington Square Pleasure Garden is supposed to be a sly nod to what were the nearby Vauxhall Pleasure Gardens, famed in the 18th century for leisure pursuits, entertainment and general debauchery.

no dogs or bicycles pleas
vote with your fag end
paris
london

05.

The Master's House, 2 Dugard Way, SE11 4TH
Kennington or Elephant & Castle tube

THE CINEMA MUSEUM

Stars in your eyes

Hidden down a cul-de-sac in Kennington is one of the world's most extensive collections of film-related images and artefacts. Fittingly, the Cinema Museum has found a temporary home in the former Lambeth workhouse where a nine-year-old boy named Charlie Chaplin and his half-brother Sydney were 'processed' in 1896.

The building was once divided into wings for men and women of 'good' or 'bad character'. Today, the musty corridors and dormitories are crammed with mechanical projectors and Art Deco cinema signs, original lobby cards, piles of periodicals dating back to 1911, and around 17 million feet of film.

This extraordinary collection was amassed by Ronald Grant, whose lifelong passion for cinema began when he helped out at his local picture house in Aberdeen as a boy. Since then, Grant has accumulated over one million cinematic images dating back to 1895, the year the Lumière brothers screened the first *actualités* in Paris. This vast anthology of production stills and portraits of movie stars keeps the Cinema Museum afloat: the images are hired out to the media. The archive is divided by subject matter, from abattoirs to ventriloquists. Leafing through the 'P' drawer, Grant offers up pictorial material on practical jokes, pratfalls, prisons and private eyes.

But it's the artefacts that really bring the early days of cinema to life. There are silent film scores and song lyrics that were projected onto the screen so that audiences could sing along as the organist played during the interval. Before X-rated movies, there was Category H: 'horrific'. There's a 1917 ticket machine that issued metal tokens of various shapes depending on the price, so ushers could feel the difference in the dark. These nattily dressed ushers would use floral sprays 'to disguise the smell of 1,000 wet raincoats and cigarettes on a Saturday night'. Cinemas may have had fancy fittings and names like the Majestic or the Picture Palace, but audiences could be rowdy. One old notice warns patrons: 'No shouting or whistling allowed – applaud with hands only. In the interests of public safety please do not spit.'

The Cinema Museum has led a precarious life, and is still struggling to maintain a permanent home here on Dugard Way. To raise funds, it has launched regular film nights and talks, held in a screening room with vintage cinema seats and illuminated signs. All proceeds go towards maintaining this glorious anachronism. A great night out for a good cause.

The Cinema Museum was threatened with expropriation in 2017 following the sale of the building, triggering a phenomenal outcry: many actors and directors, including Ken Loach, campaigned to save it, while a petition gathered over 52,000 signatures. The purchasers agreed to give the charity that runs the museum time to raise the funds needed to buy back the space housing the collection.

TODAY
PRICES OF ADMISSION
(INCLUDING TAX)
FULL
10d
STANDING
1/3
1/9 SEATS
COMING
GENTS

06.

99 Southwark Street, SE1 0JF
Waterloo, Southwark, London Bridge or Borough tube;
Waterloo, London Bridge, Blackfriars rail

KIRKALDY TESTING MUSEUM

Giant ball-breaker

This little – or not so little – gem of Victorian engineering is tucked away between the modern glass monoliths that have sprouted around Tate Modern. Opened in 1874, Kirkaldy's Testing and Experimenting Works was built to house David Kirkaldy's monstrous Universal Testing Machine: a vertical hydraulic ram, 48 feet long and weighing 116 tons, that can pull, push, bend, twist and bulge metal beams to breaking point, recording just how much pressure they can take before shattering.

Smashing things to pieces hardly feels like rocket science to 21st-century visitors, but this machine represented the cutting edge of Victorian engineering. The 19th century saw an explosion in the use of metal for construction, but designers were not always certain of the capabilities of their materials. One example was the collapse of the Tay Rail Bridge in 1879, just 19 months after it opened; the bridge's beams were tested at Kirkaldy's after being retrieved from the riverbed. On the other hand, buildings, bridges and ships were often over-engineered because their architects feared failure.

Kirkaldy introduced the greatest possible accuracy to this pioneering technology. His rigorous approach is summed up in the inscription above the workshop: 'Facts, not opinions'. Among other projects, he tested steel for the Eads Bridge over the Mississippi, one of the first steel structures in the world and still in use today, as well as materials for London's Blackfriars Bridge and Hammersmith Bridge. Originally, the works housed a Museum of Fractures, showing hundreds of different samples that had been torn apart. These are long gone, but Kirkaldy's office is still there, as well as a collection of smaller machines, including the splendidly named Cement Dogbone Briquette Machine. In the basement stands a Denison chain tester, used to find weak links – presumably best viewed at a safe distance.

If there are enough visitors, a tour of the works includes a demonstration of the giant testing machine. Tension mounts surprisingly quickly as the big beast hisses into life. The demonstrator slips an ingot of steel into the jaws of the ram and gradually cranks up the power. As the pressure rises, the ingot stretches imperceptibly. Just before its explosive failure, it sheds its coat of rust and the true metal appears beneath, before snapping loudly. Worth the admission price alone.

© Lars Plougmann

07.

Bear Gardens, Bankside, SE1 9HA
London Bridge or Southwark tube

THE FERRYMAN'S SEAT

A little seat with a long history

Wedged into a wall not far from Shakespeare's Globe Theatre, and before Southwark Bridge, is a small chunk of flinty stone. This is the last surviving example of the boatmen's seats that once lined the South Bank. Until 1750, London Bridge was the only means of crossing the Thames in central London; so 'wherrymen' ferried passengers across in narrow water taxis, or 'wherries'. The boatmen waited on these rough stone benches until their vessels filled up with rowdy patrons spilling out of the nearby Rose and Globe theatres, the bear-baiting rings and brothels (evocatively known as 'stews' because of their origins as steam baths) that littered the unsavoury suburb of Southwark.

The wherrymen must have been lean, as the seat is a tight squeeze for even the trimmest of 21st-century buttocks. It can't have been a pleasant resting place: the area reeked of open sewers and the stench of the surrounding tanneries.

BEAR-BAITING: 'A VERY RUDE AND NASTY PLEASURE'

This street is still called Bear Gardens after the Davies Amphitheatre, the last bear-baiting pit on Bankside. Banned in 1642, bear-baiting was a popular pastime in Tudor times, frequented by roughnecks and courtiers alike.

The Ferryman's Seat
The Ferryman's seat, located on previous buildings at this site, was constructed for the convenience of Bankside watermen, who operated ferrying services across the river. The seat's age is unknown, but it is thought to have ancient origins.
Historic Southwark

08.

Redcross Way, SE1 1TA
Borough tube

CROSSBONES GRAVEYARD

A burial ground for misfits

Originally a graveyard for sex workers, immigrants, suicides and other unfortunate souls not deemed worthy of burial in consecrated ground, Crossbones Graveyard continues today as a place of pilgrimage and memorial for those who still feel like outsiders.

In Medieval times, Crossbones was a graveyard for 'Winchester Geese'. In 1161, the Bishop of Winchester was granted the power to license prostitutes and brothels: this persisted for 500 years until Oliver Cromwell put an end to it. The prostitutes in this area were known as Winchester Geese, but when they died their bodies were not granted burial in the local parish. Crossbones took them in, and it continued to accept all the social misfits until 1853, at which point it was the burial site for between 15,000 and 22,000 and had become 'completely overcharged with dead'.

Crossbones was then forgotten and was only brought back to life in 1996 when a local man, John Constable, had a night-time vision of a Winchester goose who took him to the site and encouraged him to start a regular vigil for those who had been let down by society. This became a local tradition: volunteers continue to hold a vigil here at 7pm on the 23rd of every month. This ceremony honours outcasts, dead or alive. It opens and closes with a prayer and opens the floor for planned or spontaneous bardic offerings such as poems, performances or the reading of psalms.

Now owned by Transport for London (TfL), the land is managed by Bankside Open Spaces Trust (BOST) – a volunteer charity. Nature itself is given free rein to promote the idea that it is a space reserved for the unwanted. In what's called an 'outcast style of gardening', weeds and alien species are cared for and cultivated. Under BOST management, the graveyard has also become a living site and a DIY space – a constantly changing environment where visitors can bring tokens of love to memorialise people they have lost. These tokens can be anything, from written names and statues to tyres and pet toys, but most people choose to add a ribbon to the colourful iron gate.

The entrance gate is located in front of the cosy Boot and Flooger wine bar. The later is supposedly the only bar in he country not to require an alcohol license, because of special dispensation from James I in 1611.

09.

Guy's Hospital, Great Maze Pond, London SE1 9RT
London Bridge tube

KEATS STATUE

A hidden statue of John Keats in an alcove of the old London Bridge

As a place of science, the grounds of a hospital might be the last place you'd expect to find a memorial to a 19th-century Romantic poet. And yet, in a hidden courtyard of Guy's Hospital is a bronze statue of the famous writer John Keats. He is sitting in an alcove (see below), holding a book and peering out curiously at passers-by. Although this is a statue of Keats, it was actually commissioned to commemorate one of his biggest fans, Dr Robert Knight (1932–2005), who also trained and worked at the hospital.

A fact unknown even to poetry fans, Keats had a past life as a trainee surgeon-apothecary at Guy's before he decided to focus on his creative career: he started his training as a medical apprentice when he was 15. It was hard work and Southwark wasn't the nicest place to live in the Victorian period: the area around the hospital was teeming with grave-robbers and body-snatchers who would provide apothecaries like Keats with recently dead bodies for scientific examination.

Unsurprisingly, when Keats found himself 'in' with the Romantic poets set (such as Shelley, Wordsworth, Byron and other household names), he decided that the corpse-examination life wasn't for him and he left the programme.

His familiarity with medicine and healing, though, comes through in his poetry: the inscription on the long wooden panel running along the inside of the alcove reads, 'Sure a poet is a sage; a humanist, physician to all men', and is taken from Keats' epic but unfinished poem, *The Fall of Hyperion*.

In 2007 Guy's Hospital welcomed Keats back with this statue designed by Stuart Williamson. It was unveiled by the then poet-laureate and Keats biographer Andrew Motion and placed into the Old London Bridge alcove that had been in the courtyard since 1972.

AN ALCOVE OF THE OLD LONDON BRIDGE

Strangely enough, the alcove in which Keats sits once formed part of the Old London Bridge that traversed the Thames when Keats was alive. The bridge stood for 600 years before being demolished in 1832. It wasn't just a walkway: it was an iconic cultural space holding shops, houses and churches. When the bridge was widened in the mid-18th century, the alcoves were added: you can see them in Turner's 1794 painting 'Old London Bridge'. When it was dismantled, these alcoves were sold and dispersed. As well as the one in Guy's Hospital there are also two in Victoria Park in east London.

10.

9a St Thomas Street, SE1 9RY
London Bridge tube/rail

THE OLD OPERATING THEATRE

No pain, no gain

This little oddity was rediscovered by chance in 1957, during repairs in the eaves of St Thomas' Church in Southwark, on the original site of St Thomas' Hospital. This is the oldest surviving operating theatre in the country, and was used in the days before anaesthetics and antiseptic surgery. The garret also served to store the hospital apothecary's medicinal herbs. The museum that stands there now displays a collection of terrifyingly primitive medical tools, including instruments for cupping, bleeding and trepanning, a hair-raising practice of perforating the skull to 'alleviate pain.'

The operating theatre was built in 1822, after the 1815 Apothecary's Act, which required apprentice apothecaries to watch operations at public hospitals. Prior to this, operations took place in the patient's bed right on the ward, which must have been a blood-curdling ordeal – all that blood and bellowing in such a confined space. The operating theatre was annexed to the women's surgical ward, so patients could be carried straight in via what is now the fire escape. Students crammed the viewing platforms to watch the operations, carried out without anaesthetic prior to 1847. Patients, who were typically from the poorer strata of London society, submitted willingly, as this was the only way to get the best medical treatment, which they otherwise could not afford. The wealthy underwent operations in the relative comfort and privacy of their home.

OPEN SURGERY

Surgeon John Flint South described the pandemonium on the sidelines of an operation here: 'Behind a second partition stood the pupils, packed like herrings in a barrel, but not so quiet, as those behind them were continually pressing on those before and were continually struggling to relieve themselves of it, and had not infrequently to be got out exhausted. There was also a continual calling out of 'Heads, Heads' to those about the table whose heads interfered with the sightseers.'

Florence Nightingale was indirectly responsible for the operating theatre's closure. In 1859, she set up her nursing school at St Thomas', but on her advice the hospital moved to a new site opposite the Houses of Parliament in 1862. There is still a small Florence Nightingale Museum at St Thomas' Hospital (see p. 180).

MISERATIONE NON MERCEDE
REGULATIONS FOR THE THEATRE

WHITECHAPEL TO WOOLWICH

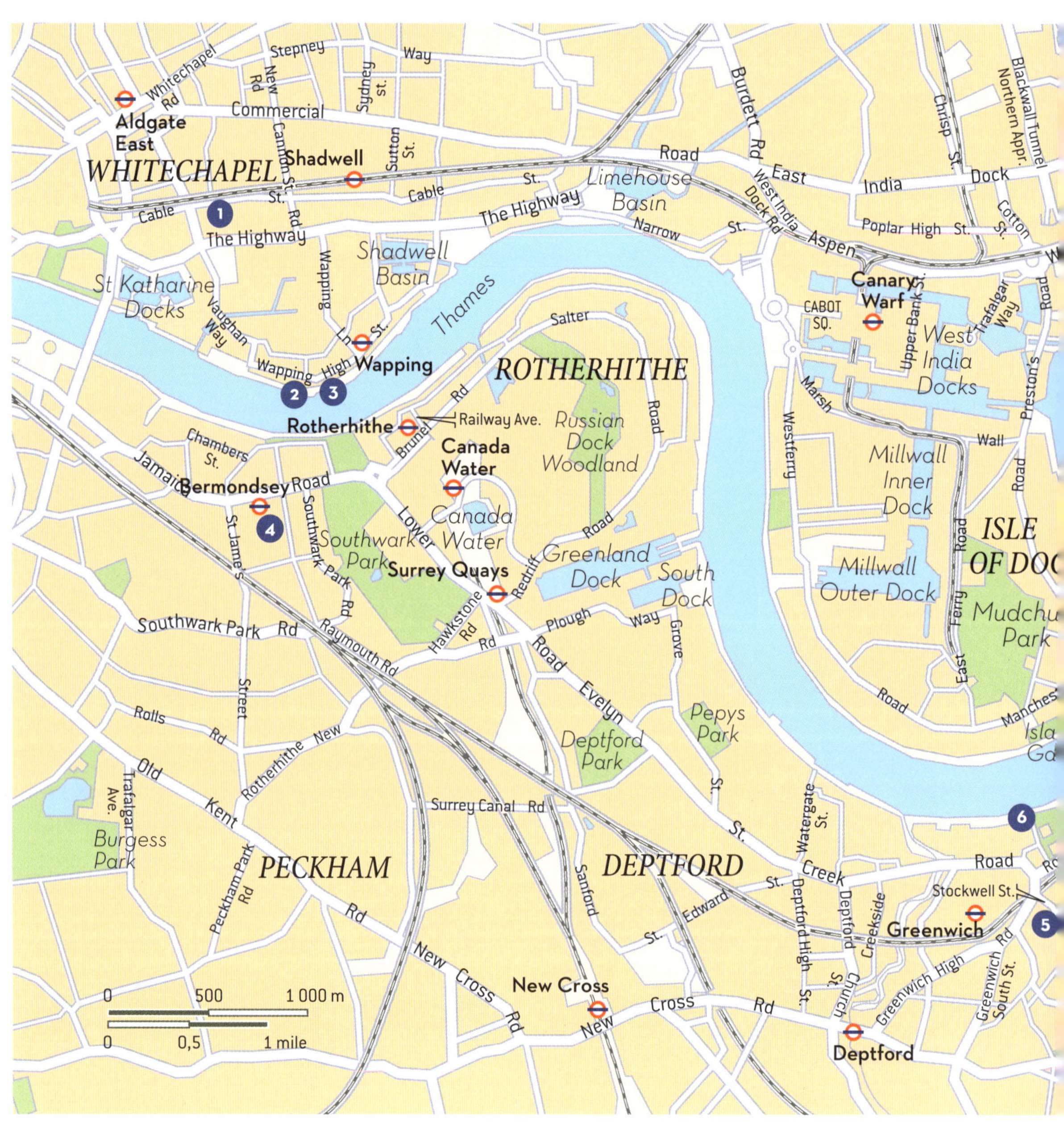

01. WILTON'S MUSIC HALL *p. 200*

02. EXECUTION DOCK *p. 202*

03. THAMES RIVER POLICE MUSEUM *p. 204*

04. PEEK FREANS BISCUIT MUSEUM *p. 206*

05. THE FAN MUSEUM *p. 208*

06. GREENWICH FOOT TUNNEL *p. 210*

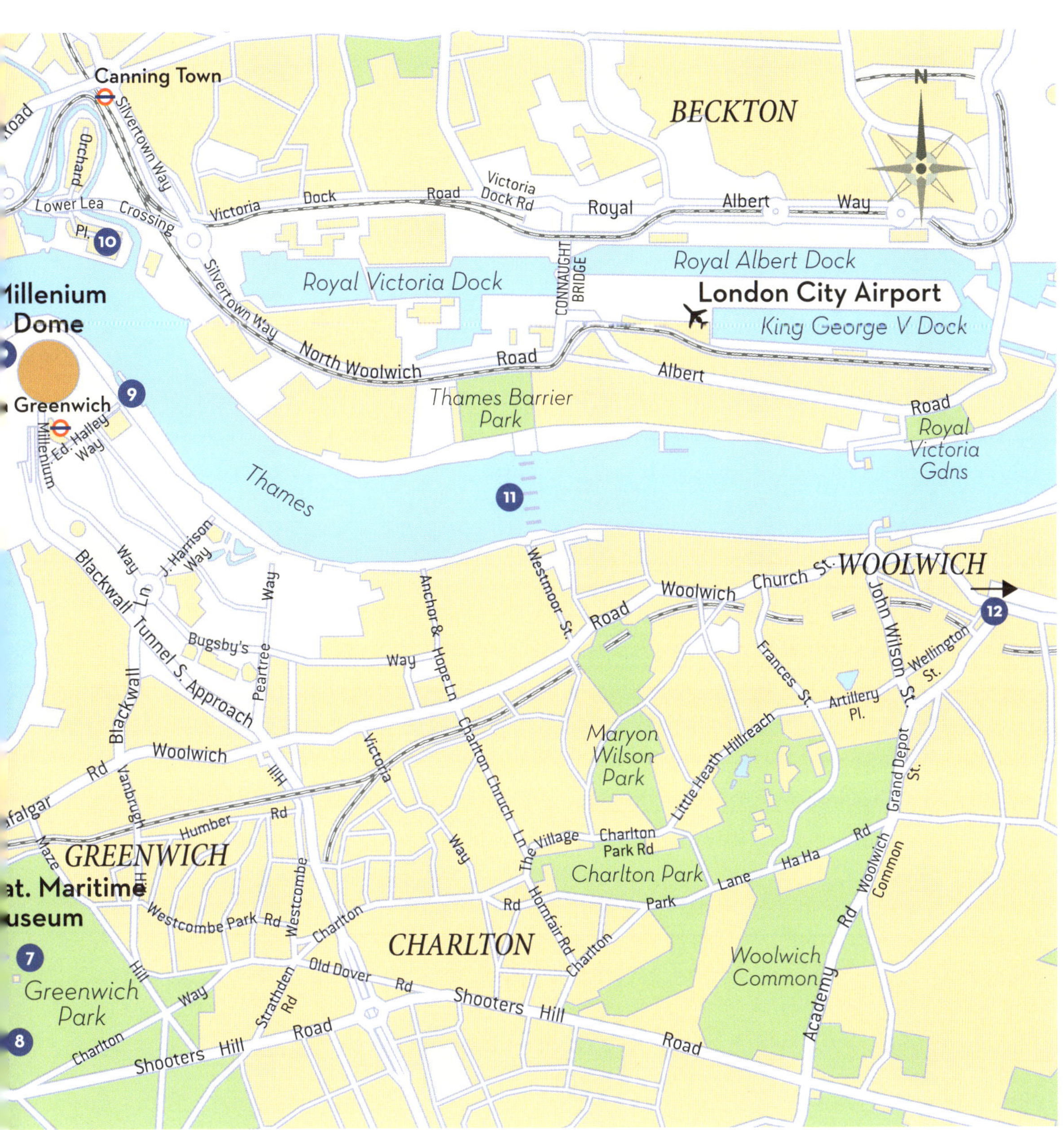
Canning Town
BECKTON
Royal Victoria Dock
Royal Albert Dock
London City Airport
King George V Dock
Millenium Dome
Greenwich
Thames Barrier Park
Royal Victoria Gdns
Thames
WOOLWICH
GREENWICH
CHARLTON
Maryon Wilson Park
Charlton Park
Woolwich Common
Greenwich Park
Nat. Maritime Museum

01.

1 Graces Alley, E1 8JB
Tower Hill tube, Shadwell DLR

WILTON'S MUSIC HALL

World's oldest surviving music hall

There is so little left of London's music halls, yet they were central to many people's lives in the capital in the days before television. These venues, popular from the early Victorian era and lasting until 1960, offered a mixture of popular songs, comedy, speciality acts and variety entertainment. Wilton's was one of the grandest.

Like many East End music halls, Wilton's was originally built as a concert venue. It stood behind a pub called the Mahogany Bar. John Wilton bought the business around 1850, enlarged the concert room three years later and replaced it with his 'Magnificent New Music Hall' in 1859. Wilton was determined to bring West End glamour, comfort and entertainment to his predominantly working-class audience and invested heavily in fitting out a 'sun-burner' chandelier of 300 gas jets and 27,000 cut crystals that illuminated a mirrored hall. He also installed the best available heating, lighting and ventilation systems and strove to make sure that the acoustics in the hall were perfect.

Some of the biggest stars of the day performed here, including George Ware (writer of the song, 'The Boy I Love is Up in the Gallery'), Arthur Lloyd and George Leybourne, better known as Champagne Charlie. Part of Leybourne's schtick included living the life of a swell on and off the stage – this involved the consumption of plentiful free champagne from wine merchants looking to promote themselves. Leybourne died of liver disease aged 42.

Wilton's was only a music hall for 30 years. It was destroyed by fire in 1877, was rebuilt and then became a mission of the Methodist Church for nearly 70 years. It then became a warehouse, but was scheduled for demolition as part of the slum-clearance schemes of the 1960s. A campaign was started to save the building, with supporters including John Betjeman, Peter Sellers and Spike Milligan, and it reopened as a theatre and concert hall in 1997. The place has an elegantly decayed feel to it and shows off its scars beautifully.

WILTONS
WILTON'S
PUSH TO ENTER
WILTONS

WILTON'S

02.

Wapping Old Stairs, off Wapping High Street, E1W 2PN
Shadwell DLR, then 15-minute walk, or Wapping Overground

EXECUTION DOCK

Where timbers were shivered

London's connection with piracy is hardly surprising, given the city's history as one of the world's greatest ports. Pirate life seems to have been pretty desperate, despite all the fighting and drinking; pirate death seems to have been even worse, either killed in action, or more likely by picturesque diseases (Vomito Negro? Flux? The Itch? Yellow Jack?). Worst of all was to be dispatched at Execution Dock.

Policing the sea was left to the Admiralty, and for 400 years it executed pirates on the foreshore of the Thames at Wapping, at a site far enough offshore as to be near the low-tide mark. Typically, prisoners were publicly executed en masse after being paraded from the Marshalsea Prison across London Bridge and past the Tower of London.

The hanging was unusual in that the rope was too short for the drop to break necks, so the condemned would 'dance' as they strangled. Their bodies were left in place until three tides had washed over them. The more notorious corpses were then tarred and hung in cages along the Thames estuary to encourage other sailors to behave themselves. Captain Kidd, inspiration for Robert Louis Stevenson's Treasure Island, stepped off here, and George Davis and William Watts were the final two hanged for piracy at the docks on 16 December 1830.

The actual site is disputed, as the gallows are long gone; three pubs on Wapping High Street claim it as an attraction. The Prospect of Whitby, London's oldest riverside pub formerly known as the Devil's Tavern, is one, the Captain Kidd another; but the likeliest location is behind the Town of Ramsgate. Go down the alley at the side, descend Wapping Old Steps and you are on the river bed (obviously wait until the tide is out). Walking on the foreshore is well worth it; the river is constantly turning up weird flotsam and jetsam. However, to actually dig you need a special licence from the Port of London Authority.

MUDLARKING

Sounds like a filthy habit, but mudlarking is actually the word used for beachcombing along the Thames – named after a bird, apparently. Access to the river is surprisingly easy (especially along the south bank), either through ancient water-steps such as Pelican Stairs or down modern steps from the Embankment. The highlight of the mudlark's year is the annual opening of the beach in front of the Tower of London in conjunction with National Archaeology Week.

03.

Wapping Police Station, 98 Wapping High Street, E1W 2NE
Wapping Overground

THAMES RIVER POLICE MUSEUM

The world's first police force

London is home to the world's first police force. Established in 1798, the Thames River Police were recruited by the West India Merchants and Planters Committees to protect their cargo from river pirates. Magistrate Patrick Colquhoun had worked out that half a million pounds' worth of freight was being filched each year. The original force had about 50 members: watermen, who rowed the boats; surveyors, who checked cargo; and lumpers, who supervised the offloading of vessels. Armed with cutlasses, pistols and truncheons, they had to monitor the 33,000 workers on the Thames, a third of whom – according to Colquhoun's calculations – were felons. In its first year of operation, the river police saved £122,000 worth of cargo.

The force was absorbed into London's Metropolitan Police in 1839. Now known as the Marine Support Unit, high-speed launches have replaced the rowing galleys and officers are more concerned with counter-terrorism than brigands. But the 78-strong force still operates from the original police station on Wapping High Street. The workshop where boats were repaired was converted into a museum in 1974. Visitors are treated to an expert commentary by curator Robert Jeffries, a retired marine policeman and City of London guide.

Motorised launches were introduced after the 1878 Princess Alice disaster, in which 640 day-trippers died after two ships collided. The Thames is now one of the cleanest rivers in Europe, but back then most of the passengers were killed by swallowing raw sewage. The ship's tattered ensign is on display in the museum, a gift from the captain's son, who joined the river police soon afterwards.

There is an impressive collection of handcuffs, uniforms, telescopes and rattles, used before whistles to sound the alarm. The most remarkable objects are the 18th-century handwritten ledgers, detailing everyday crimes and punishments. The first page of a tattered inspector's pocketbook from 1894 details the discovery of a baby's severed head in the Thames. Most of the policemen's misdemeanours involve drinking on duty. Some 30 pubs lined the riverbank in Wapping, including the Turk's Head, where those condemned at nearby Execution Dock (see previous double page) could enjoy their last pint.

THE ORIGINS OF POLICE STATIONS

The term 'police station' derives from the police craft 'on station' (anchored) at various points in the Thames. The phrase 'on the beat' comes from the beating of the oars in river police boats.

POLICE
STATION
20

04.

100 Drummond Road, SE16 4DG
Bermondsey tube

PEEK FREANS BISCUIT MUSEUM

A hidden but very welcoming museum dedicated to the confectionary company that created the Bourbon biscuit

Locked away on one of the top floors of the old Peek Freans biscuit factory is a tiny museum dedicated to the confectionary company that created the Bourbon biscuit. Finding the museum would be impossible without help: you first need to get through a gated entrance, up a vault-like lift, down a private corridor and into a locked room. Which is why visitors must arrange private visits via email.

Yet despite all the security, this is one of the most welcoming museum experiences you'll find in London, with hands-on curators Gary and Frank providing a wealth of knowledge, guided tours and complementary tea and biscuits.

The museum is made up of two rooms filled to bursting with biscuit memorabilia. You can trace the change in biscuit-tin design through the ages, from the mirrors, paintings and book covers that adorned the luxury tins of the nineteenth century to the gaudy flower boxes of the 1960s. You can have a go at opening the 'magic casket', play with the biscuit-tin puzzles or listen to the biscuit-tin music boxes. There are even some biscuits preserved in their original packets from 1934 although they are certainly not to be nibbled at.

Without a doubt the *pièce de résistance* is a true-to-life model of the 600-lb wedding cake that Peek Freans gifted to Queen Elizabeth on her wedding day to Prince Philip in 1947. The original was six tiers, made from ingredients donated by members of the Commonwealth, and was topped by a solid silver icon of St George about to slay a dragon. When Peek Freans sent the cake off to the wedding party, they also created a model to display at their factory reception. Unhappily, the model was destroyed by vandals and in 2015 the museum re-created the model with the help of the British Sugarcraft Guild.

To ensure that the decorations on the replica cake were accurate, a team at Warwick University volunteered to create 3D silicone models of the original panels. The Sugarcraft Guild then used these models to handmake the embellishments, so everything you see on the cake is made of royal icing. Everything except St George and the dragon: this is a 3D printed model of the original, made possible by the Royal Collection, which allowed the original silver figure to be laser scanned so it could be printed and added to the top tier. The re-creation of the cake was a feat of modern engineering and traditional craft, and it was finished just in time for the couple's platinum wedding anniversary in 2017.

05.

12 Crooms Hill, Greenwich SE10 8ER
Greenwich rail/DLR, Cutty Sark DLR

THE FAN MUSEUM

Miniature masterpieces

The Fan Museum in Greenwich is another of London's many specialist museums reflecting the obsessive, collecting side of the English. It claims to be the only museum in the world devoted to every aspect of fans and fan making (although a similar venture exists in Paris), and there may be good reason for this – the craft does seem limited. But the collection works as a set of miniatures and the building itself is worth visiting. Housed in a pair of listed Georgian buildings from 1721 that have been restored to their original state, the museum contains over 3,500 mostly antique fans from around the world. These date from the 11th century to the present day. However, the bulk of the collection is based around fans from the 18th and 19th centuries, when mass production of folding fans saw their use spread throughout society. Demand was such that the fan makers had their own livery company, which still exists, although its membership now mainly derives from the heating and air-conditioning industry.

Fans may be practical objects, but the blank canvas of the 'leaf' meant that they became a highly decorative form of display. Fans often directly referred to contemporary events and allegiances, with Nelson's victories a particularly popular subject in mass-produced fans. They also served as a kind of primitive advertising hoarding. At the fancier end of the market, leading society artists painted fans for clients – the museum holds a fan painted by Walter Sickert. The functions of the fans on display thus vary wildly: ceremonial tools, fashion accessories, status symbols, political flags, or advertising giveaways.

On the first Saturday of the month, the Fan Museum holds fan-making workshops.

FAN LANGUAGE

The practical use of a fan is clear. However, at the apogee of their popularity at the turn of the 19th century, a whole language was involved in their use, much of which can be seen in contemporary paintings. A fan resting upon the lips, for example, means 'I don't trust you'; placed on the heart it declares, 'My love for you is breaking my heart'; hiding the sunlight implies that 'You are ugly'; and fanning with the left hand says, 'Don't flirt with that woman'. Go to the museum, buy a fan, and reinstate these practices in polite society.

06.

Cutty Sark Gardens, Greenwich / Island Gardens, Isle of Dogs
Island Gardens or Cutty Sark DLR

GREENWICH FOOT TUNNEL

Tunnel under the Thames

The Greenwich Foot Tunnel, an underwater passageway linking Cutty Sark Gardens in Greenwich and Island Gardens on the Isle of Dogs, is one of the great engineering feats of 19th-century London. Lined with 200,000 glazed white tiles, which give it the unfortunate acoustics and ambience of a public toilet, the tunnel opened in 1902. Designed by Sir Alexander Binnie, it was commissioned to alleviate the overcrowded ferry service used by commuters who worked at the docks on the Isle of Dogs. Once barely populated, the marshy Isle of Dogs grew with the success of the British Empire. By the end of the 19th century, the population had risen to 21,000. International shipping poured into the new docks, which once stretched all the way from Tower Bridge to Barking, making London the largest port in the world. All of this is long gone. The Isle of Dogs still maintains its reputation as one of the tougher parts of town, but 'The Docklands' is now synonymous with the executive housing that services the City of London to the west and Canary Wharf to the east.

The entrance shafts at both ends of the tunnel are topped by glazed cupolas. Lifts (not running at night) and spiral staircases allow pedestrians access to the tunnel, which is 370 metres long, with an internal diameter of about three metres. The tiled walls make the tunnel echo eerily, especially when you creep into it in the dead of night – the tunnel is a public highway and therefore by law is open 24 hours. At such times of low traffic, it feels like the loneliest, most desolate place in London, until the sound of approaching heels ring down the tunnel like bullets.

HIDDEN RIVER CROSSINGS

Greenwich Tunnel is actually the third tunnel constructed under the Thames. The Thames Tunnel, designed by Brunel, opened in 1843. It came to be regarded as the haunt of prostitutes and 'tunnel thieves' who lurked under its arches and mugged passers-by. Greenwich Tunnel was duplicated about three miles downstream at Woolwich Crossing, which runs between Silvertown and Woolwich, one of the few areas in London to escape gentrification. The ferry across the river is also a treat. Unlike any of the other boats on the Thames, the ferry crossing here is free, and gives an idea of the river's scale.

07.

Royal Observatory, Blackheath Avenue, Greenwich Park, SE10 8XJ
Cutty Sark DLR, Greenwich or Maze Hill rail

STARGAZING AT THE ROYAL OBSERVATORY

Secrets of the stars

The Royal Observatory in Greenwich Park may have been designed for surveying the stars, but the views of London from this hilltop landmark are equally spectacular. The dazzling towers of Canary Wharf and the distant glow of the London Eye are most dramatic at night, but the park closes at dusk. To enjoy this view – and see the stars, too – book a place on one of the Royal Observatory's special 'Evenings with the Stars'. These are held in the autumn and winter – check online for availability from September.

After an illuminating zoom into the night sky overhead in the high-tech Planetarium, with live commentary from one of the resident astronomers, visitors climb up a tower crowned with a bulging dome. As E. Walter Maunder wrote in 1900: 'This dome – which has been likened according to the school of aesthetics in which its critics have been severally trained, to the Taj at Agra, a collapsed balloon, or a mammoth Spanish onion – houses the largest refractor in England, the 'South-east Equatorial' of twenty-eight inches aperture.'

This colossal feat of Victorian engineering is still the UK's largest refracting telescope. Built by Sir Howard Grubb in 1893, it took eight years to complete and weighs 1.4 tons. The lens alone weighs 102 kg. The telescope is tilted parallel to the Earth's axis of rotation, so you can follow a star from east to west by simply rotating the mount. This isn't quite as clever as it seems: the mount doesn't actually fit inside the dome. Despite the addition of a GPS system, moving the telescope involves cumbersome manoeuvres of the dome's retractable shutters and crawling about on the floor. Early astronomers often had to lie flat on the floor to look through the lens. What you see depends on the time of year and the weather. The experience will be enjoyable even if it's overcast, as enthusiastic astronomers explain the mysteries of the solar system and point out stars with fantastical names, from Aspidiske to Zubenelgenubi.

MERIDIAN LINE LASER

As the official starting point for the New Millennium, a bright green laser was turned on at the Royal Observatory in December 1999, illuminating the path of the Prime Meridian Line across the London sky. It is visible for 10 miles on a clear night.

08.

Near Chesterfield Gate in the southwest corner of Greenwich Park, entrance from Charlton Way, SE10 8QY
Blackheath or Greenwich rail, then bus 53, 386

PRINCESS CAROLINE'S SUNKEN BATH

Bubble trouble

In 1795, Princess Caroline of Brunswick married her cousin George, the Prince of Wales (later King George IV). It was not a happy marriage. Fat George (known as Prinny) was pressured into marrying Caroline and secure the succession as part of a deal to get his massive debts cleared by the government, and had, in fact, already (secretly and illegally) married his mistress, Maria Fitzherbert. On first sight of Caroline, George staggered off to the other end of the room and said to the Earl of Malmesbury: 'Harris, I am not very well, pray get me a glass of brandy'. He then spent the next three days before the wedding drinking, and collapsed into the bedroom fireplace on the wedding night.

Not an auspicious start. The philandering prince started spreading rumours about Caroline's sluttish and slovenly ways – apparently, she was adulterous, never washed, rarely changed her underclothes, and had bad breath because of her fondness for raw garlic and onions.

After giving birth to a daughter, the couple were formally separated and Caroline went to live in Montague House in Greenwich, where she allegedly consoled herself with wild orgies and scandalous affairs. When Caroline finally tired of Britain and went into self-imposed exile in 1814, in a fit of pique George had Montague House torn down. The site is now part of Greenwich Park.

Between the Ranger's Lodge and the Rose Garden, however, a little piece of Caroline's pleasure palace survives: a sunken bath complete with a staircase. Used as a flowerbed for decades, the white-tiled plunge pool was unearthed in 1909. A small plaque commemorates the scorned princess, proving that although she may have been unfaithful at least she wasn't unhygienic.

09.

Thames Path (by the Millennium Dome), Greenwich Peninsula, SE10
North Greenwich tube

'SLICE OF REALITY' AND 'QUANTUM CLOUD'

Radical riverside sculptures

The Millennium Dome may have been a failure in its initial function (a glorified big top, dreamed up by politicians), and the estimated £1 billion development costs makes its current use as a concert venue hard to stomach. The tube station that serves it, North Greenwich, was money better spent: the blue-tiled and glazed interior and raking concrete columns were designed by Will Alsop, and merits a visit in their own right.

In addition to the Dome, the government also threw cash at artists to create municipal art in the surrounding area. Two of the most successful results are right by the river and are easily viewed from the Thames Path. (This stretch is best accessed from Greenwich proper; the short walk reveals the Thames as a more obviously tidal river.)

'Slice of Reality' is by Richard Wilson, a sculptor who works with volume. His most famous work is 20:50, a room half-filled with sump oil that leaves the viewer feeling like they are embedded in a liquid black mirror. 'Slice of Reality' is equally disorientating: a 20-metre-high cross-section of a 600-ton dredger set in the Thames riverbed. Seen at low tide, the sculpture looks as though it will keel over from its dainty little plinth. The effect close up is unnerving – only 15% of the ship remains, yet the slice overwhelms. It serves admirably as a memorial to the maritime past of London.

'Quantum Cloud' is by Anthony Gormley, probably the most high-profile creator of public art in Britain. At first sight, this giant work appears to be a cloud created by thousands of square, hollow sections of steel. Focus, and at the centre of the cloud the outline of a human form emerges. The river as a backdrop makes perfect sense; the sculpture appears to echo the whirling seabirds of the Thames and the static form is full of movement.

These two sculptures now form part of The Line, London's first dedicated contemporary art walk. The route runs between the Queen Elizabeth Olympic Park and The O2, following the waterways and the Meridian line (the-line.org). Work in the immediate vicinity of the Dome includes Alex Chinneck's playful 'A Bullet from a Shooting Star', an inverted electricity pylon. Other attractions along the walk include Damien Hirst's 'Sensation', installed at Cody Dock.

10.

Trinity Buoy Wharf, 64 Orchard Place, E14 0JY
East India Dock DLR, then 10-min walk

LONGPLAYER

Music for a millennium

Housed in London's only lighthouse, Longplayer is probably the most protracted celebration of the third millennium. Launched on January 1, 2000, this musical installation features a composition for Tibetan singing bowls and gongs, digitally remixed so that the same sequence of sounds will not be repeated for 1000 years. On December 31, 2999, Longplayer will return to its starting point – and begin all over again. That is, as long as the technology that powers it survives or evolves, or some very dedicated musicians volunteer to perform the score in perpetuity.

Creator Jem Finer, a founding member of The Pogues, is exploring the possibility of building six two-armed turntables 6 to 12 feet in diameter, with automated mechanisms to raise and lower the arms. Even if Finer figures that out, he will have to build a device capable of cutting 12-foot records. A likelier solution is a dedicated global radio frequency, or a 'small computational device' along the lines of those used in deep space missions. The possibility of endless live performance is also being explored.

Listening to this mesmerising soundscape in a disused lighthouse, with views across the Thames to the docks and the Dome, is both captivating and slightly creepy. Built in 1864, Trinity Buoy lighthouse was used to develop lighting for Trinity House, an association founded in 1514 to safeguard shipping and seafarers. Its headquarters are still located in the city (trinityhouse.co.uk).

CONTAINER CITY

Trinity Buoy Wharf was named for the wooden buoys made and stored here in the early 19th century. Urban Space Management, using the huge metal shipping conatiners that helped kill off London's docklands, built the first prototype Container Cities here in 2000 and 2002. They consist of stacked, recycled containers, whose brightly coloured, corrugated walls and porthole windows conceal low-cost studios and homes for a community of artists and designers. Most of them open their studios for Open House weekend. A few more containers have been sound-proofed and can be hired as music studios.

11.

1 Unity Way, Woolwich, SE18 5NJ
Charlton or Woolwich Dockyard rail, or North Greenwich tube, then bus 161 or 472

THAMES FLOOD BARRIER

High and dry

About 8 miles downstream from Tower Bridge is the Thames Flood Barrier, a row of ten movable gates across the river that protect London from flooding. The effect is that of ten gleaming sails moving upstream, line abreast. On a sunny day, viewed from the river or the shore, they are a pleasingly modern feature in an otherwise run-down part of London. Measuring 520 metres wide, the flood barrier consists of a set of semi-cylindrical gates that rotate upward from the riverbed, closing the river to traffic. When closed, the four largest gates stand as high as a five-storey building.

The need for the flood barrier seems to escape most Londoners, who prefer not to think about the implications of its construction. But the barrier has been raised 176 times since 1982, and the frequency is rising. Global warming and rising sea levels are partly responsible for a rise in tide heights in the Thames, while the movement of tectonic plates in the Mid-Atlantic Ridge is gradually causing South East Britain to sink seaward. The wide mouth of the River Thames and its position at the foot of the North Sea also make the river vulnerable to surge tides. The construction of the Embankment has constrained the swollen river even more tightly – witness the height of the Thames during high tide at Blackfriars Bridge. So when the river siren sounds, run for the hills.

The Information Centre on the south bank contains a working model of the barrier and exhibits about its construction and the Thames. There are good views of the Barrier from the café. Also worth a look is the Thames Barrier Park, 14 hectares of public space built on what was one of the country's most polluted sites, the former PR Chemicals factory.

Access to the barrier is a little awkward. It is best viewed as part of a walk along the Thames Path, which stretches 184 miles from the river's source in Gloucestershire. Pick up the trail by the Cutty Sark in Greenwich and walk downstream past the Millennium Dome to the barrier. Then press on to Woolwich, cross the river by ferry or foot tunnel, and catch a train back into central London from North Woolwich.

8
9

12.

The Crossness Engines Trust, Thames Water S.T.W., Belvedere Road, SE2 9AQ
Abbey Wood rail. On Steaming days, a minibus usually operates from Abbey Wood to the Crossness site every 30 mins. Otherwise it's a brisk 30-minute walk from the station through an industrial wasteland

CROSSNESS PUMPING STATION

Healer of the Great Stink

There aren't many opportunities to make a trip to a sewage farm, but Crossness Pumping Station – opened in 1856 by Edward, Prince of Wales – offers the chance. The obsolete Pumping Station is located in the middle of the Crossness Sewage Treatment Works, which is still very much operational: if you miss the shuttle service from the station, simply follow your nose.

The Pumping Station was part of legendary engineer Joseph Bazalgette's innovative sewage system for London. By the mid-19th century, London's exploding population meant the Thames had effectively become an open sewer. The contaminated water caused cholera outbreaks that killed over 30,000 Londoners. Plans to address this were finally put into action following the 'Great Stink' of 1858, when an unusually warm summer and clogged-up River Thames made the House of Commons unusable. Bazalgette built 1,100 miles of brick-lined, underground sewers that diverted untreated sewage downstream.

Crossness was the business end of the southern half of the system (a similar station at Beckton performs the same function for North London). Sewage arrived at the site and was pumped up into a 17-foot-deep reservoir, which could hold 27 million gallons of waste. The reservoir gates were opened twice a day, and the contents were swept out to sea on the Thames' ebb tide. Eventually, only liquid waste was disposed of in this way; the prosaically named 'sludge boats' dumped solid, untreated waste beyond the mouth of the river until 1998.

Crossness Pumping Station is an incredible place. The Beam Engine House, home to four steam-driven pumping engines, contains some of the most spectacular ornamental ironwork in the capital. At the heart of the building is the Octagon, an exuberant framework for the engines made of brightly coloured iron columns and screens. This is characteristic of the Victorians' love of Gothic adornment in the unlikeliest places.

The building was abandoned in the 1950s after it became obsolete. Ongoing restoration work, largely by unpaid volunteers, began in 1987. The scale of the engineering is unnerving: the four engines (each weirdly named after a member of the royal family) are the largest rotative beam engines in the world. They have 52-ton flywheels and 47-ton beams, and were capable of pumping around 20 milk lorries of sewage a minute into the reservoir. Only one – the 'Prince Consort' – is currently restored, but the Crossness Engines Trust is now focused on bringing 'Victoria' back to her former glory.

GREATER LONDON (NORTH)

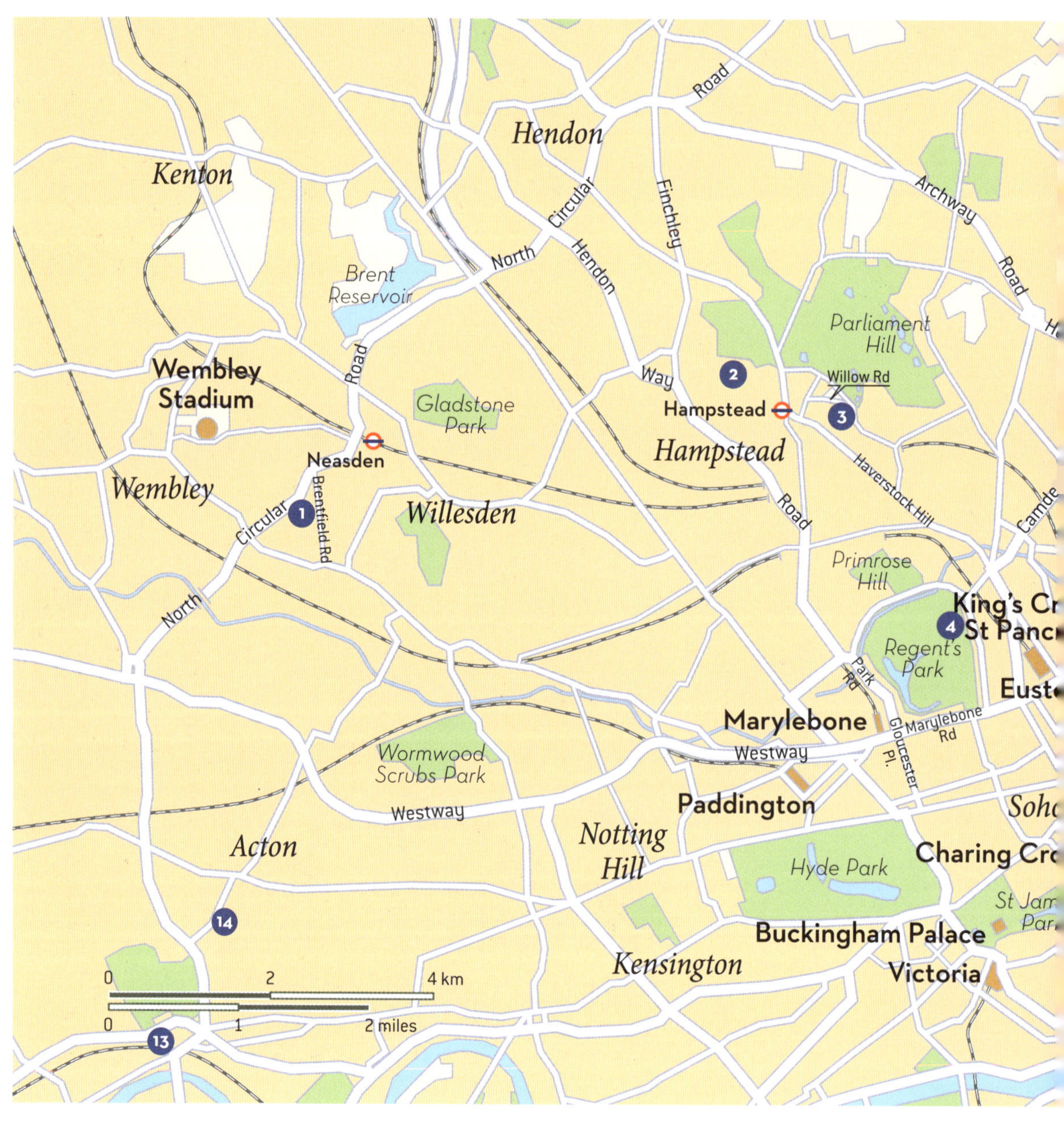

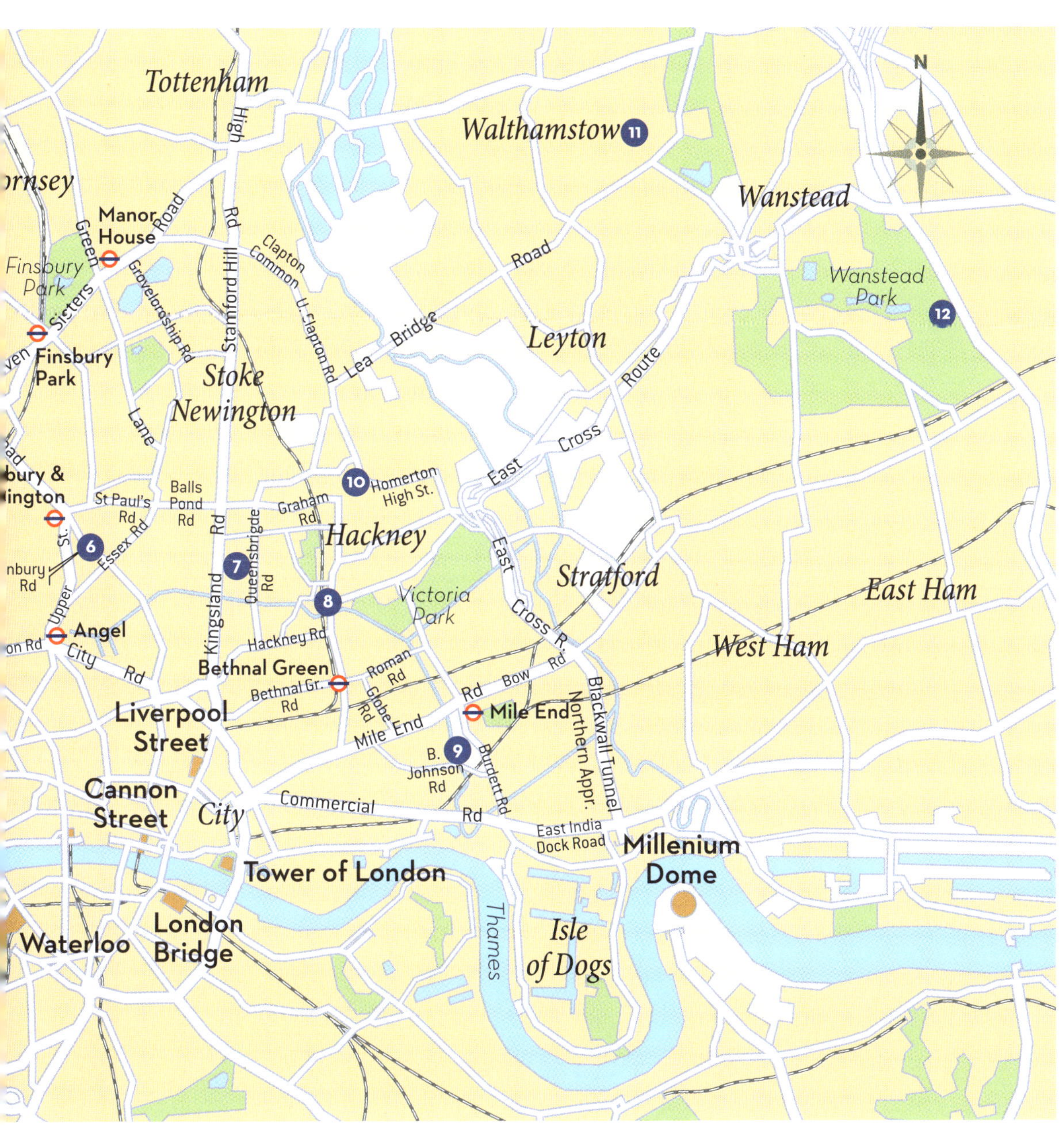
N
Tottenham
Walthamstow
11
Wanstead
Wanstead Park
12
Manor House
Finsbury Park
Stoke Newington
Leyton
Hackney
10
Homerton High St.
6
7
8
Victoria Park
Stratford
East Ham
West Ham
Angel
Bethnal Green
Mile End
Liverpool Street
9
Cannon Street
City
Tower of London
Millenium Dome
London Bridge
Waterloo
Thames
Isle of Dogs
Lea Bridge Road
East Cross Route
Commercial Rd
East India Dock Road
Blackwall Tunnel Northern Appr.
Kingsland Rd
Stamford Hill Rd
Clapton Common
U. Clapton Rd
Graham Rd
Hackney Rd
Roman Rd
Bow Rd
Mile End Rd
Burdett Rd
B. Johnson Rd
Globe Rd
Bethnal Gr. Rd
City Rd
Upper St.
Essex Rd
St Paul's Rd
Balls Pond Rd
Queensbridge Rd
Green Lane
Seven Sisters
Grosvenor Rd

01.

Pramukh Swami Road, Neasden NW10 8HW
Neasden tube

BAPS SHRI SWAMINARAYAN MANDIR

Neasden Nirvana

Scarcely believable at first sight, this is the largest Hindu temple outside India. This spectacular edifice was opened in August 1995 by His Holiness Pramukh Swami Maharaj. It is but a stone's throw from the grim North Circular, the drab ring road circling London's northern suburbs. To build it, 5,000 tonnes of Indian and Italian marble and Bulgarian limestone were hand-carved into 26,300 pieces by 1,526 skilled craftsmen in India, then shipped to London and assembled like a giant jigsaw puzzle in less than three years. The finished building includes seven shikhars (or pinnacles), six domes, 193 pillars, and 55 different ceiling designs.

Deities and motifs representing the Hindu faith spring from the walls, ceilings and windows. The heart of the mandir, or temple, is its murtis, or sacred images of the deities, who are revered as living gods. In total, there are 11 shrines with 17 murtis, including Ganesh, Hanuman, and Swaminarayan – to whom the temple is dedicated. The deities are ritually served by dedicated sadhus (monks) who live in the temple. Before sunrise, the murtis are woken by the sadhus and the shrine doors opened for the first of five daily 'artis' (prayers). Feeding and bathing of the murtis continues throughout the day. The best time to visit is just before 11.45am, when the rajbhog arti ceremony is performed daily. Lit candles are waved in front of the embodiments of the deities, accompanied by a musical prayer performed by drums, bells, gongs and a conch-shell. A haunting and uplifting experience.

02.

Hampstead Grove, Hampstead, NW3 6RT
Hampstead tube

FENTON HOUSE

Comfortable country house

Few people seem to know of or visit this large, well-appointed National Trust property near Hampstead tube station. As a result it has the feel of a trip to the countryside, despite its central location.

Dating from 1686, it was bought by merchant Philip Fenton in 1793. The house remained largely untouched over the years; it has a huge walled formal garden, a rose garden, a kitchen garden and a 300-year-old orchard. Apple Weekend, held every year in late September, gives members of the public the chance to try old English varieties of apples.

The garden is worth the trip alone. However, the house's real glory is the interior. In 1936, the house was bought by Lady Katherine Binning, who filled the house with her collections of porcelain, 17th-century needlework pictures (known as stump work) and Georgian furniture. Lady Binning lived alone in this pile – and very comfortable she made it too – before bequeathing it to the National Trust following her death in 1952. Subsequent additions include an impressive collection of paintings, notably a selection of the Camden Town Group of English Post-Impressionists, which includes work by Walter Sickert. Elsewhere, paintings by Sir William Nicholson also stand out.

In the attic there is a painting of Mrs Jordan, the Irish actress who bore the Duke of Clarence ten illegitimate children. He shamefully abandoned her once he had a sniff of the throne and was crowned as William IV. His portrait hangs in the hall, next to his appalling brother, George IV. One of William's daughters also lived in the house for a while.

If harpsichords are your thing, the Benton Fletcher Collection of Early Keyboard Instruments is also worth a look. The house hosts musical events exploring different aspects of these instruments.

03.

2 Willow Road, Hampstead NW3 1TH
Hampstead tube or Hampstead Heath rail

2 WILLOW ROAD

A modernist show home

Ernö Goldfinger is most famous as the architect of Trellick Tower, a 1960s high-rise council block in West London, once as notorious for brutal crimes as its Brutalist design. Trellick Tower is now a listed building, where small flats come with sky-high prices. The first house the Transylvanian émigré ever built was this low-key, low-rise Hampstead home, where he lived with his family for almost 50 years.

What makes this modernist show home unique is that everything is exactly as Goldfinger designed it in 1939 – and exactly as he left it on his death in 1987, from the prototype door handles on his desk to the baked beans in his wife Ursula's kitchen. The house is as fascinating for its ingenious, daring design as its insight into Goldfinger's life and work. The art collection is impressive, too: works by Bridget Riley, Max Ernst, and Marcel Duchamp hang alongside Ursula's surrealist paintings. In the 1930s, rural Hampstead had replaced Chelsea as the epicentre of a lively, left-wing arts scene. Lee Miller, Roland Penrose, and Henry Moore attended the Goldfingers' glamorous parties.

Although the house is relatively small – at least by Hampstead standards – folding doors, hidden storage, and vast windows with unbroken views of Hampstead Heath create a sense of space and light. Passionate volunteers offer guided tours several times a day. A graceful spiral staircase (designed by Ove Arup) leads to a lacquered scarlet landing. The house's Cubist colour palette – midnight blue, tomato red, mustard, terracotta – is oddly soothing. The furniture – mostly designed by Goldfinger himself – still looks thoroughly modern. The house faced intense opposition when it was built. Goldfinger, who retorted that 'only the Eskimos and Zulus build anything but rectangular houses', was forced to cover the concrete frame in brick cladding to blend in with its Georgian neighbours. One of the main objectors was the Tory Home Secretary, Henry Brooke. Ironically, it was his son, Peter Brooke, then Heritage Secretary, who took possession of the house on behalf of the National Trust. Goldfinger's children could not afford the whopping death duties.

GOLDFINGER'S NASTY NAMESAKE

By all accounts, the dashing Goldfinger was a difficult man, mitigated by his generosity and charisma. But the anti-Semitic author Ian Fleming took such a dislike to Goldfinger's radical designs and Marxist principles that he named his infamous Bond villain after him. When the real Goldfinger threatened to sue Fleming's publisher, the author offered to change his character's name to Goldprick.

04.

Regent's Park Inner Circle, NW1 4NR
Regent's Park, Great Portland Street, Baker Street, St John's Wood & Camden Town tubes

FOSSILISED TREE STUMPS

Botanical specimens that might be 100 million years old

There's a corner of the Inner Circle of Regent's Park that takes you back all the way to the Cretaceous Period. Laden with ferns, trees and a cascading waterfall, this section of the landscape holds the ecological life of our ancient past. But some items are literally from this ancient past: hidden among the plants are botanical specimens that could be up to 100 million years old – they are the ancient trees of Regent's Park, or more accurately, the ancient tree stumps.

How these stumps appeared in the gardens remains a mystery. It is thought that the Royal Botanic Society brought them over in the 19th century when they leased the Inner Circle from the Crown and created their own botanic garden. The Society's aim was global science and they used the land to grow and study plants. Members would travel all over the world collecting seeds and plants and, apparently, tree stumps. Brought back to England, these specimens would be studied in the name of knowledge. Although you might think that the stumps were scouted from the ends of the earth, it is now believed that the trees were originally a grove of conifers from Dorset.

PETRIFIED TREES

The trees in Regent's Park Inner Circle have survived so long because they are 'petrified'. This odd term describes the phenomenon whereby a tree's organic material is replaced by minerals, so that it is gradually turned into stone.

Although we don't know quite how this happens, there is another famous fossilised tree stump displayed outside London's Natural History Museum which can tell us more: 330 million years old, it was excavated from a quarry in Edinburgh.

It seems the pressure of lying beneath the quarry deprived the tree of oxygen so it couldn't grow, but water flowing through the sediment deposited minerals in the cells, slowly shifting the organic balance.

After being buried underground for such a long time, the tree bark was described as 'so hard as to strike fire with steel'.

05.

12/13 New Wharf Road, N1 9RT
King's Cross tube/rail

THE ICE WELLS OF THE CANAL MUSEUM

The history of London's waterways

Today, stolen bicycles and supermarket trolleys clog London's murky canals. But until the 'great freeze' of winter 1963 finally killed off commercial canal traffic, barges cruised these waterways weighed down with bulk cargo of all kinds. London's network of canals remained the cheapest means of transporting goods across long distances well after the arrival of railways. Regent's Canal was built in the early 19th century to link the Grand Junction Canal at Paddington with the Docklands. At first, canal boats were drawn by horses, but a steam tug was introduced in 1826. By the 1840s, there was talk of turning the canal into a railway, but luckily this never happened.

Converted from an old ice-house used to store ice imported from Norway, in the days before refrigeration, the London Canal Museum is an old-fashioned, offbeat little venue that tries to capture this forgotten history. Some details are slightly cheesy – a fake horse, clothed dummies – but you can nose around a reconstructed narrowboat decorated with traditional roses and castles patterns, and peer down into the impressive ice wells, where hundreds of tons of ice were stored.

From the canalside terrace, spot the cranes and loading doors where barrels of Guinness were unloaded at the bottling factory on the other side of Battlebridge Basin, now transformed into trendy offices.

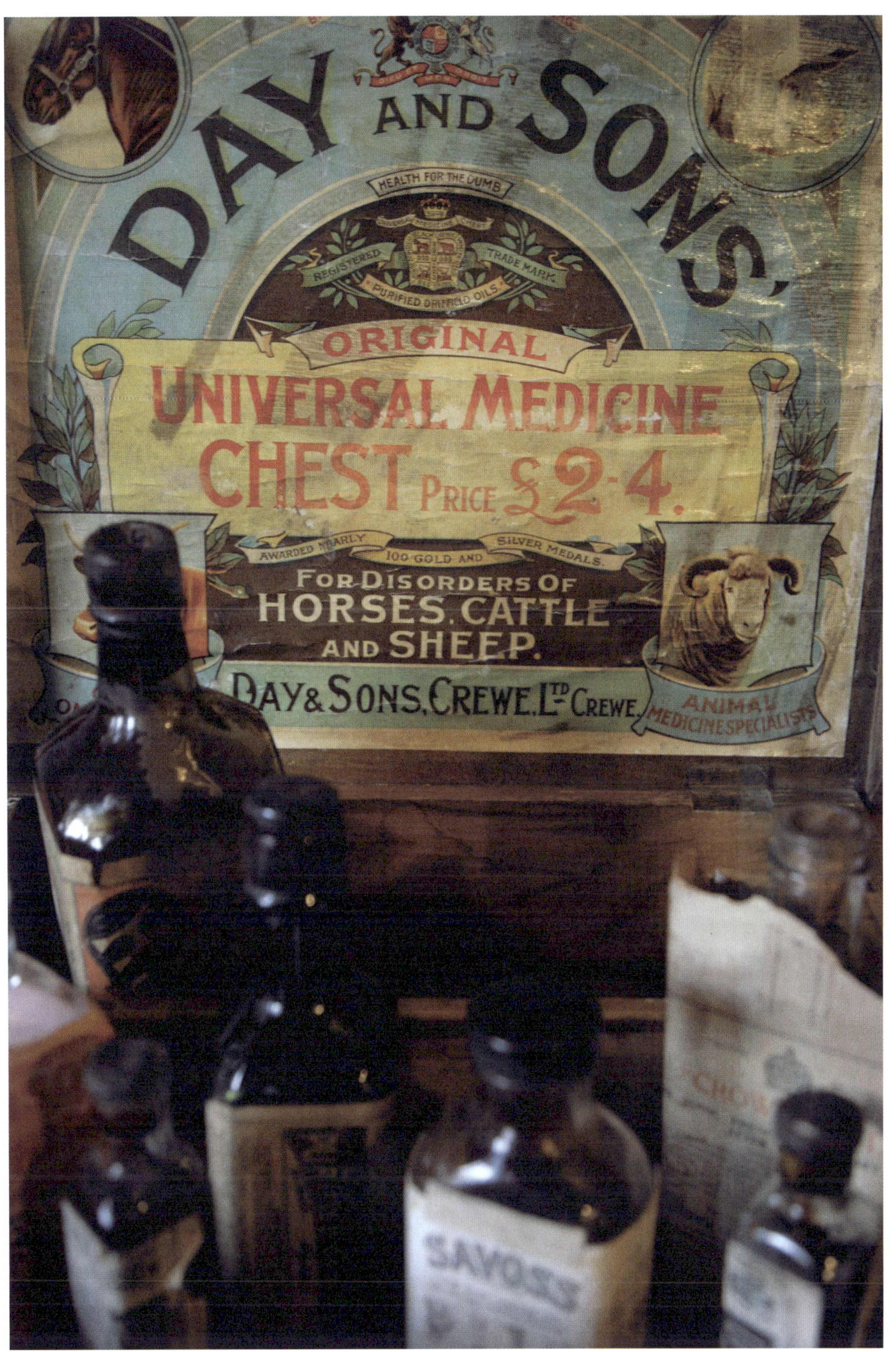
DAY AND SONS'
HEALTH FOR THE DUMB
REGISTERED
TRADE MARK
PURIFIED DRIFFIELD OILS
ORIGINAL
UNIVERSAL MEDICINE
CHEST PRICE £2-4.
AWARDED NEARLY
100 GOLD AND
SILVER MEDALS.
FOR DISORDERS OF
HORSES, CATTLE
AND SHEEP.
DAY & SONS, CREWE. L^TD CREWE.
ANIMAL
MEDICINE SPECIALISTS

06.

Canonbury N1 2PU. The best entry point is on Canonbury Road
Essex Road or Canonbury rail, Highbury & Islington tube

NEW RIVER WALK

Last trickle of a great waterway

With its Georgian mansions built around leafy squares, Canonbury is one of the lushest and loveliest corners of London. Only developed as a residential area in the early 19th century, Canonbury retains the feel of an exclusive country retreat. Running through the vast – and vastly expensive – houses of Canonbury Grove is a little stream, hidden from view by weeping willows and luxuriant shrubbery. This sleepy waterway is one of the last remaining sections of Hugh Myddelton's New River, an aqueduct built in 1613 to bring drinking water from springs in Hertfordshire to a reservoir in Myddelton Square, near Sadler's Wells.

Before 1600, London's water supply was sourced from the River Thames and local streams, wells and springs. Often contaminated, water was distributed by sellers sloshing wooden buckets. Hugh Myddelton, a goldsmith and serial entrepreneur, persuaded King James I to cover half the costs of creating a 39-mile aqueduct, on condition the King received half the profits and that the waterway ran through his palace grounds at Theobalds. Over 200 labourers were paid the equivalent of 4p a day to dig out the New River. The water was channelled throughout the city through hollowed out elm trunks. Although the aqueduct still supplies about 8% of London's water, most of the New River has been covered over by buildings.

Created in 1954 and maintained by volunteers from the Canonbury Society, New River Walk meanders for about a kilometre through fragrant gardens crossed by wooden footbridges. Water is pumped upstream to preserve the effect of a moving river. Hungry herons and ponderous ducks drift along the mossy surface of the shallow waterway. After your stroll, refresh yourself with a pint and a roast at the exceptionally cosy Myddleton Arms, named (but misspelled) after the self-taught engineer.

07.

Holy Trinity Church, Beechwood Road, Dalston E8 3WD
(entrance on Cumberland Close)
Dalston Junction Overground

CLOWNS' GALLERY AND MUSEUM

Fool's paradise

The Holy Trinity has been London's Clowns' Church since 1959. The only clue to this curious association is a stained-glass window in the main hall, depicting scenes from the life of Joseph Grimaldi (1778-1837), the godfather of all jesters. In a tiny room at the rear of the church (accessed via Cumberland Close) is one of London's smallest museums: the Clowns' Gallery. Over a tinkling soundtrack of fairground tunes, a clown/curator entertains visitors to the monthly open day with uproarious anecdotes. Among the clown stamps, cartoons and tributes are a few religious references to 'The Holy Fools': a tapestry proclaiming 'Here we are fools for Christ' and The Clown's Prayer (a slightly cloying ode to laughter). The real highlight is the collection of clown portraits painted on over 200 porcelain eggs. A tradition that originated in the late 1940s, these eggs are faithful representations of the trademark make-up worn by each clown – a suitably humorous way of patenting their personal face-paint. In addition to paint, the artist uses samples of each clown's costume and wig to produce an 'eggs-act' miniature portrait.

Traditionally held at Holy Trinity, but recently relocated to All Saints Church on nearby Livermere Road, the annual clown service takes place on the first Sunday in February. Among the local congregation in their Sunday best, a 'pratfall' of clowns in full 'motley and slap' cause havoc in the pews – blowing bubbles, honking horns, wearing stilts, and singing along to 'Send in the Clowns'. One popular hymn at the Holy Trinity goes like this: 'When we are tempted in our pride to dizzy heights of sin, beneath our feet, oh Lord, provide a ripe banana skin...' Get there early – the clown service is always packed.

JOSEPH GRIMALDI, THE GODFATHER OF CLOWNING

Joseph Grimaldi, who made his debut at Sadler's Wells aged three, pioneered many modern clowning techniques, from visual pranks to the dreaded audience participation. A blue plaque marks Grimaldi's former home at 56 Exmouth Market, Clerkenwell. His grave is largely overlooked in the grubby little Joseph Grimaldi Park on the corner of Pentonville Road and Rodney Street, Islington. With a happy and sad mask dangling from the iron railings, it's a rather forlorn tribute to the fools' hero, but every June a lively festival is held here in Grimaldi's honour.

08.

11 Mare Street, E8 4RP
Cambridge Heath or London Fields rail, Bethnal Green tube

MUSEUM OF CURIOSITIES

The beautiful and the damned

'Those easily offended by death and decay should stay away.' Don't say you haven't been warned: the Museum of Curiosities is not for the faint-hearted. (Another sign on the door, pinched from druggie dandy Sebastian Horsley's Soho front door, reads: 'This is not a brothel. There are no prostitutes at this address.')

Descending a gold spiral staircase into the musty basement, it takes a while to adjust to the crepuscular gloom. Beasts, freaks and monsters gradually start swimming into view: a two-headed kitten, a unicorn's skull, a tongue-eating louse, a mummified pygmy, pickled babies in bottles. Alongside the taxidermy and totems peering from the walls and ceilings are glass cabinets crammed with erotica ('small pecker condoms'), juvenilia (celebrity poos) and occult paraphernalia (a sinister alchemist's toolkit). Perhaps the weirdest item of all is 'a casket containing some of the original darkness that Moses called down upon the earth'. There's a corner devoted to artist Stephen Wright (see p. 280) and a shrine to Horsley, including a red glitter suit and the nails he used to crucify himself.

Most objects are labelled with spidery black captions that might have been written by Prince Charles, but are in fact the handiwork of Viktor Wynd, the collector and curator of this singular *Wunderkabinett*. A self-styled 'artist, author, lecturer, impresario and 'pataphysicist' (the apostrophe is deliberate; the quasi-philosophy is best defined as a bunch of pretentious provocateurs), Wynd made a name for himself on the London underground scene, hosting masquerade balls and literary salons. All the while, he was amassing this private collection of the grotesque and macabre, creepy and shocking, sublime and ridiculous. It began as a curiosity shop and gallery, but achieved museum status thanks to a crowd-funding campaign. If you have anything at home you think Wynd might like, do post it to him at the museum.

The admission price includes a cup of tea at the bar upstairs, a faintly sleazy affair crammed with skeletons, skulls and stuffed animals. Absinthe cocktails, edible insects and chocolate anuses are consumed at your own risk. Occasionally, you might stumble into a taxidermy class or a seance, so it's probably best to ring ahead of your visit.

09.

46–50 Copperfield Road, E3 4RR
Mile End tube or Limehouse DLR

RAGGED SCHOOL MUSEUM

A Victorian lesson in East End history

Tower Hamlets is still one of the poorest boroughs in London, but in Victorian times it suffered poverty on an incomparable scale. Families were crammed into one-room flats and illiterate kids ran barefoot along the coal-blackened alleys. One third of all funerals in the area were for children under five. When Thomas Barnardo arrived in London in 1866 to train as a missionary, a cholera epidemic had swept through the East End. Barnardo set about founding the Ragged Schools to provide free education for London's poorest children. Today, kids can dress up like Oliver Twist at the Ragged School Museum, a Dickensian throwback aptly located on Copperfield Road in Mile End.

From 1887 to 1908, tens of thousands of children were educated at this school, housed in a former warehouse beside Regent's Canal. On the first Sunday of every month, a Victorian lesson is re-enacted by a suitably severe actress in period costume (accessorized with a forbidding cane) in one of the original classrooms. Scratched desks with inkwells, slate writing boards, and dunce hats create an evocative setting for this local history lesson. Kids are encouraged to be hands-on: sitting at the desks, climbing into the tin bath, or getting to grips with a mangle and carpet beater in the Victorian kitchen.

Downstairs is the small Museum of Tower Hamlets, which offers a potted history of local landmarks like the Bryant and May match factory, now converted into luxury flats. There are mementoes from the Blitz, including song sheets with jaunty titles like 'In the Blackout Last Night', designed to boost wartime morale. Visitors can learn about other well-meaning Victorian institutions like the Working Lads Institute, whose mission was to teach young workers to read and write, and The Factory Girls Club, run by 'refined Christian ladies' to teach girls 'feminine and domestic virtues' so they could become servants.

The promise of free meals led to overcrowding in the Ragged Schools, although school dinners were just as dire in those days: 'Breakfast was bread and cocoa. Dinner was lentil or pea soup and bread, varied occasionally by rice and prunes or haricot beans.' Threatened with demolition in the early 1980s, the building was converted into a museum after a campaign by local residents. Barnardo's is still one of the UK's biggest children's charities.

25th July 1888
ABCDEF
GHIJKLM
NOPQRST
UVWXYZ

10.

2 & 4 Homerton High Street, E9 6JQ
Hackney Central rail

SUTTON HOUSE

The oldest house in Hackney

Once the last bastion of pre-hipster Hackney, even Homerton has been gentrified; soon there will be more flat whites than fried chicken shops.

In Tudor times, Homerton was so upmarket that dozens of aristocrats built country estates here. Thomas Sutton, supposedly the richest commoner in Britain and founder of Charterhouse, lived in Homerton. This National Trust property is mistakenly named after Sutton; in fact, he lived next door in a mansion that has since been demolished.

Sutton House's mish-mash of architectural styles reflects its motley succession of residents since 1535. The original owner, Sir Ralph Sadleir, Henry VIII's Secretary of State, had 30 acres of gardens and orchards attached to Bryk Place, the only brick building in what was then a half-timbered village. The cellar contains stacks of 500-year-old bricks, hand-made in situ from blood red 'brickearth' drained from nearby Hackney Brook.

Sutton House has successively been occupied by a sheriff, a silk merchant, a girl's school (coyly known as The Ladies' University of Female Arts), a church institute, and trade union, until it was bought by the National Trust in 1938. Not much happened until the 1980s, when a bunch of punks squatted the derelict building – a perfect venue for underground gigs and raves.

Miraculously, many of the original Tudor features survived: oak-panelled rooms, carved fireplaces, a flagstone courtyard, and an authentically rudimentary kitchen. The Linenfold Parlour is the most impressive room, lined with wood panels carved to look like draped fabric. Bizarrely, this panelling was stolen in the late 1980s, but later sold back to the National Trust.

Visiting Sutton House is like going on a historical treasure hunt. You can lift floorboards, open panels, and peer inside cupboards to discover traces of the house's hidden past. Poke your nose into the Victorian garderobe, or toilet – people hung their clothes in the loo, believing the stench of ammonia would keep moths away. Kids can rummage through period costumes or explore a caravan retro-fitted like a stately home in Breakers Yard. Traces of a 17th-century trompe-l'œil mural are far more accomplished than the wall paintings daubed by punks in the attic, which contains what looks like the prototype of Tracey Emin's unmade bed. But the squatter's slogans couldn't be more topical: 'London belongs to the millions, not the millionaires.'

11.

Unit 12, Ravenswood Industrial Estate, Shernhall Street, E17 9HQ
Walthamstow Central tube, Wood Street rail

GODS OWN JUNKYARD

The light fantastic

Like so much of London, Soho is being sanitised. One by one, the salacious sex shops and seedy drinking dens are being swallowed up by bland restaurant chains and overpriced cocktail bars. Bar Italia is still hanging on, its neon clock luring late-night drinkers for a shot of espresso. And there are still a few peep shows on Brewer Street, their lurid signs advertising the presence, behind tinsel curtains, of girls, girls, girls.

Soho's saucy signage is the legacy of lighting designer Chris Bracey, who died in 2014, aged 59. Bracey's dad, Dick, a Welsh miner, moved to London after the Second World War and landed a much less gloomy job as an electrical engineer for funfairs and amusement arcades. In 1952, he set up Electro Signs, London's first neon sign maker, in Walthamstow. Dick Bracey quickly spotted the commercial potential of Soho's red light district: he installed illicit signs outside sex shops in the dead of night, enlisting his young son, Chris, as his partner in crime.

Electro Signs is still in business. A few streets away, hidden on a drab industrial estate, Chris Bracey set up his own neon emporium in 2005. Squeezed between a car mechanic and a microbrewery, Gods Own Junkyard is part workshop, part showroom. As well as Bracey's own creations, it contains the biggest collection of vintage neon signs in Europe.

Like some kind of psychedelic discotheque, every inch of the shambolic warehouse is aglow. There are flaming lips and flickering hearts, flashing slogans ('Sex, drugs and bacon rolls') and retro signs for pawnshops and massage parlours. A wooden shed has been converted into a tongue-in-cheek shrine, with statues of Buddha and a Catholic priest framing a life-size Jesus with a fluorescent halo, packing a pair of blue neon pistols. The work is called 'Son of a Gun'.

After vajazzling Soho's fleshpots, Bracey branched out to create brilliant backdrops for several blockbusters, including 'Blade Runner' and 'Batman'. Not surprisingly, Gods Own Junkyard – still a family concern, run by Bracey's wife, Linda, and sons, Marcus and Matt – has itself featured in fashion and film shoots. Discovering this technicolour wonderland in the depths of suburbia is still an eye-popping surprise. After admiring the eye candy, you can have tea and cake in the secret garden, where tiny tables are topped with giant toadstools.

YOU
The CAVERN CLUB
APPLAUSE
FRANK

12.

Wanstead Park, E11 2LT
Wanstead Park tube

WANSTEAD GROTTO

Aladdin's grotto

Wanstead Grotto is a place of strange magic. Spotted from across the lake, hidden by trees and reeds and now covered by a protective net, the crumbling stone walls and high arches could be straight out of a Gothic novel. Hard to believe, but these walls were once decorated with the most dazzling jewels, fossils and crystals that money could buy. The grotto was built in the grounds of Wanstead House, one of London's grandest 18th-century homes, and was used as a 'curiosity' for guests, acting as a place of entertainment and leisure to demonstrate the wealth and style of the owners. The grotto cost the Earl of Tylney around £2,000 to build (£300,000 in today's currency) but with the the ostentatious interior design, the final value reached a whopping £40,000 (£5 million today). Grottos and follies were fashionable at the time as the ultimate leisure location. Wanstead Grotto had a boathouse on the ground floor with a chamber above it, embellished with a stained-glass window and a mirror-paved floor. Over the years it was used as a boat dock, keeper's accommodation, theatrical staging and a place of entertainment. Wanstead House was demolished in the 1800s but the grotto survived and was opened to the public, who were enchanted with the hidden cove. Tragically, they only had two years to enjoy the grotto before it burnt down in a fire caused by an unattended, overflowing pot of boiling tar. To make matters worse, the lake had been drained that year, so there was no water nearby to put the fire out – the firemen had to bring water all the way from the River Roding, some distance away, to extinguish the flames. The façade was saved but the interior was badly damaged. After this disaster, the grotto was abandoned and overrun by nature: a few years ago, you wouldn't have been able to see the stone underneath all the moss. The Heritage of London Trust and the Friends of Wanstead Parklands have now taken over conservation: plans are underway to assess the damage, remove the plant growth and rebuild the walls.

13.

399 High Street, Brentford, TW8 0DU
Kew Bridge rail

THE MUSICAL MUSEUM

Feel the Mighty Wurlitzer

Music is something we take for granted these days; the stuff pours out of headphones, video games, restaurant toilets and lifts. We've reached this stage in a series of short, rapid steps, and this purpose-built museum is full of the baroque miracles that got us here. Founded by Frank Holland in 1963, this is one of the world's foremost collections of automated music systems. This means machines you might be familiar with – musical boxes, pianolas, iPods – and machines you might not. The Hupfeld Phonoslizst-Violina, anyone?

What's most impressive about the museum is that the trust responsible for it aim to get as much as possible of the collection up and running; for this reason, it's essential to check the timings for a guided tour with instrument demonstrations. Working highlights include a rudimentary German jukebox the size of a Transit van, a coin-operated violin player and king-sized gramophones. The ambition of the builders of these machines is impressive – an orchestrion, for example, was designed to replicate the sound of a small orchestra using actual instruments, and sounds like twenty musicians trapped in a box. The sophistication of what were almost entirely mechanical devices is amazing – some player pianos, which slid over a piano keyboard and were operated by foot, were able to reproduce the nuances of the artists who recorded the musical rolls they used. And the guide will let you have a go on one if you're good.

But the glory of the museum lies sleeping in its own hall on the second floor. One of the main uses of these instruments was to accompany silent films. The grander the cinema, the grander the accompaniment, and grandest of all was a Wurlitzer, a massive organ which not only played music, but also produced sound effects including rain, birdsong and storms. The museum's Wurlitzer came from the Regal Cinema in Kingston on Thames; it can play itself, but in its day was often played by leading cinema organists who were stars in their own right.

MONTHLY TEA DANCES AND SILENT FILMS ACCOMPANIED BY THE WURLITZER

The museum runs monthly Tea Dances accompanied by the Wurlitzer, which include a free dance class and a glass of prosecco, as well as occasional concerts. More excitingly, it runs seasons of the type of silent films it was designed for. On these nights, the Mighty Wurlitzer is woken, and rises up from the floor, lights blazing and pipes howling, to thrill audiences all over again.

14.

118–120 Gunnersbury Lane, Acton Town, W3 9BQ
Acton Town tube

LONDON TRANSPORT MUSEUM DEPOT

London Transport's attic

This is a treasure trove for the train spotters, bus lovers and assorted public transport perverts who live in London, of whom there are a surprisingly large number. The London Transport Museum in Covent Garden is a restrained, well-thought-out collection of highlights from the city's history of public transport; the Depot, which houses over 320,000 items that make up the bulk of the museum's collections, is something else. It's hard to imagine that a warehouse of 6,000 square metres might be bursting at the seams, but the Depot – which contains full-length tube trains and a large collection of buses and trams, as well as all the ephemera that go with running them – certainly feels like it might pop at any moment.

There is a huge variety of things to see. Admittedly, some of this is fairly specialist – a large number of what could be electricity transformers from Frankenstein's laboratory at the entrance, for example – but much of it is immediately accessible. The extensive collection of architect's models includes the maze of passenger tunnels at Oxford Circus. There are, of course, hundreds of station signs using the famous roundel that show how it evolved, maps and even a cabinet containing the famous Johnston Sans typeface, displayed like a holy relic in a glass case. There are oddities, too – a fragment of the experimental spiral escalator at Holloway Road looks like a terrible idea, but it was built anyway. At times, it feels a bit like a house-clearance sale, but the glory of the depot is the machinery. There are some recent tube trains – London Underground is in the middle of replacing rolling stock across its network – but the bulk are vehicles from the past. They include a first-class carriage from 1892 that spent many years as a chicken coop before being fully restored; it was used to carry passengers during the celebrations for the Underground's 150th anniversary in 2013. The enormous Leyland charabanc, a predecessor of the coach, is crying out to be driven. In fact, you walk around wishing that London Transport could bring most of the collection back into use – the trams, the buses with their conductors, the trolley buses. For a Londoner, what's interesting is the instant familiarity of much of the collection despite its being long out of use, presumably a reflection of innate style.

© Colin Smith / London Transport

GREATER LONDON (SOUTH)

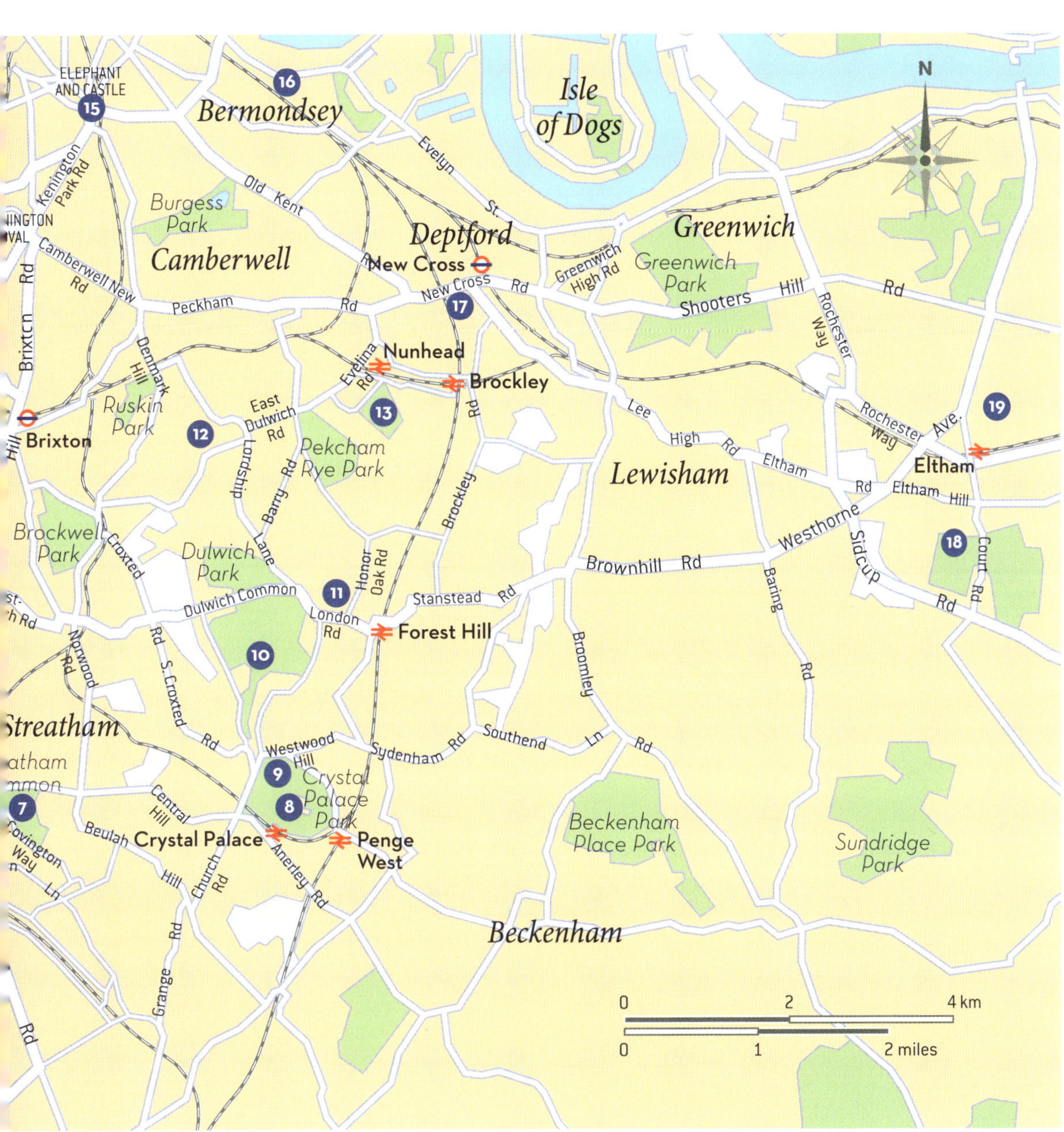

N
ELEPHANT AND CASTLE
Bermondsey
Isle of Dogs
Evelyn St.
Kennington Park Rd
Old Kent
Burgess Park
Camberwell
Deptford
New Cross
Greenwich
Greenwich High Rd
Greenwich Park
Shooters Hill Rd
Camberwell New Rd
Peckham Rd
New Cross Rd
Brixton Rd
Denmark Hill
Nunhead
Evelina Rd
Brockley
Rochester Way
Rochester Way
Ave.
Ruskin Park
East Dulwich Rd
Lee High Rd
Eltham Rd
Brixton
Pekcham Rye Park
Lordship Lane
Barry Rd
Brockley Rd
Lewisham
Eltham
Eltham Hill
Brockwell Park
Croxted
Dulwich Park
Honor Oak Rd
Westhorne
Sidcup Rd
Court Rd
Brownhill Rd
Baring Rd
Dulwich Common
Stanstead Rd
London Rd
Forest Hill
Norwood Rd
S. Croxted Rd
Bromley Rd
Streatham
Westwood Hill
Sydenham Rd
Southend Ln
Crystal Palace Park
Central Hill
Beulah Hill
Crystal Palace
Penge West
Church Rd
Anerley Rd
Beckenham Place Park
Sundridge Park
Grange Rd
Beckenham
0 2 4 km
0 1 2 miles

01.

Crane Park, Whitton, TW2 6AB
Whitton rail or Richmond tube/rail, then H22, 110 or 111 bus

CRANE PARK SHOT TOWER

Blast from the past

London was once full of munitions works, most of which were at a good distance from the centre, as they had a nasty habit of exploding. Standing alone in the middle of Crane Park is the last remnant of the Hounslow Gunpowder Mills – its shot tower. The mills once ran along the River Crane, a Thames tributary that flowed into the river at Isleworth. Its isolation was perfect for the frequently lethal manufacture of weapons.

The Hounslow Gunpowder Mills went up spectacularly at regular intervals, including one explosion in 1772 that blew out all the stained glass at Horace Walpole's country house, Strawberry Hill, over 4 miles away. There were plenty of fatalities over the years, and the last recorded explosion was in 1915.

The Shot Tower, built in 1826, is the last intact structure of the factory, which was in operation until 1927. The tower was used to make ammunition: lead was melted in a crucible at the top of the tower, forced through a copper form to gauge the bullet size, and then dropped down through the inside of the tower. As the drops fell, surface tension drew them into spheres. At the bottom, they were caught and cooled in water. Anything that failed to make the grade was returned to the top of the tower to start again.

The Crane Park tower is a small one, only capable of making bore shot. Some of the millstones used to grind saltpetre, an ingredient of gunpowder, lie at the foot of the tower. The millpond has been turned into a nature reserve, where, if you look carefully, you can still see some traces of the munitions industry, including blast mounds, sluice gates and engine beds. The Shot Tower, which contains information about the surrounding wildlife reserve, is only open to the public on Sunday afternoons.

Ammunitions factories were once a huge industry supplying the British Empire. The biggest was the Royal Arsenal in Woolwich, which employed 80,000 workers during the First World War. The arsenal has, predictably, been converted into riverside flats, but you can explore its explosive history at the Greenwich Heritage Centre (greenwichheritage.org), housed in the old ordnance factory.

02.

Herbarium and Library, Kew Gardens, Richmond TW9 3AE

HERBARIUM OF THE ROYAL BOTANIC GARDENS

Seven million dried plants locked away in cupboards

An old Victorian building located just outside the high brick walls of the famous 300-acre botanic gardens, Kew's Herbarium might be the most important place you've never heard of. It's dedicated to discovering all the secrets of the plant kingdom.

Described as a 'vault', the three-storey gallery rooms are piled high with cupboards upon cupboards filled with over 7 million dried plant specimens used for scientific research. If you open one of the temperature-controlled cupboards, you'll see various folders stacked on top of one another. Each folder contains a dried plant specimen, information about where it was found, who donated it to Kew and details about the species. These specimens are used to uncover the inner workings of the natural world and provide the basic material for scientists to experiment with medicines, clothes and food.

Looking at the hundreds of cupboards, thousands of files and millions of plants, it's astonishing to think that there's any kind of order, but these collections are systematically arranged down to the minutest detail. Plants are grouped together in different 'families' [e.g. pea-family, *Fabaceae* in Latin], 'genus' [e.g. pea, *Pisum*] and 'species' [e.g. garden pea, *Pisum sativum*]. This makes it easier for researchers to find a particular species but, because our understanding of plants is constantly changing, the location of each specimen isn't set in stone. With each new scientific discovery, the collections are evaluated and might have to be rearranged depending on the latest research.

The oldest specimen dates from 1699 and there are still many mysterious specimens that haven't been identified. These plants must wait for a new scientific discovery before they can be catalogued and find a home in the vault.

The Herbarium was built in 1877 to hold the samples that botanists sent back from their global travels. Filled with exotic tokens from the adventures of Charles Darwin, Alfred Russel Wallace and Richard Spruce, the collection (and the whole building) has been expanding ever since, with around 30,000 new additions every year, sent in parcels through the post from around the world.

03.

St Mary Magdalen Roman Catholic Church
61 North Worple Way, Mortlake, SW14 8PR
Mortlake rail

RICHARD BURTON'S MAUSOLEUM

A tent in a graveyard

Richard Burton is buried in a tent near East Sheen. No, not that Richard Burton – the film star is still buried in Switzerland. This is the far more interesting, far stranger Richard Burton, the Victorian explorer, geographer, translator, writer, soldier, orientalist, cartographer, ethnologist, spy, linguist, poet, fencer, diplomat and reputed speaker of at least 29 languages.

Burton was one of those 19th-century supermen who seemed able to turn his hand to anything. He is best known as the translator and publisher of unexpurgated versions of 'The Arabian Nights', the 'Kama Sutra' and 'The Perfumed Garden' (the 'Kama Sutra''s Arab equivalent) in English, scandalising Victorian England, and for his attempt to discover the source of the Nile, which almost killed him.

Although Burton sounds like the archetypal Victorian hero, in fact he was critical of the colonial policies of the British Empire, putting his career at risk. He was also pretty eccentric. While in the army (where he was nicknamed Ruffian Dick), he kept a troupe of monkeys in the hopes of learning their language. He had himself circumcised to sneak into Mecca in disguise. He challenged someone to a duel for making fun of his moustache. Later in life, he worked on a hypothesis that homosexuality was determined by geography. His interest in sexuality allegedly led him to measure the penises and record the sexual practices of the locals wherever he travelled. He wrote a monograph entitled 'A History of Farting'.

So, a live wire. His energy bursts out of the photographs of him, even in old age. His wife Isabel was no slouch either – a writer and philanthropist who learnt to fence in order to accompany him, she designed their tomb. The design is supposed to reflect Burton's deep ties with the Arab world. It is (very) loosely modelled on a Bedouin tent, and is decorated with a frieze of Islamic stars and crescents, as well as a crucifix and Star of David. Unlike a Bedouin tent, you can go round the back, climb up a short ladder and peer into it through a window, where the couple's coffins are on display side by side.

The church itself is a bit hard to find – be careful not to confuse it with nearby St Mary the Virgin, a far likelier looking place for the Burtons' tomb.

04.

17 Lifford Street, SW15 1NY
Putney Bridge or East Putney tube

THE ANTIQUE BREADBOARD MUSEUM

Look at my lovely bread

You've heard of a micro-brewery? A small brewer, focused on lovingly made artisanal beer? Well, this is a micro-museum, one room in Madeleine Neave's home devoted to lovingly made wooden breadboards.

A museum dedicated to the most ordinary item in a kitchen may sound dull, but nothing is ever really boring or ugly, it's all a question of how carefully you're prepared to look at it. And the Antique Breadboard Museum lets you look carefully, and as a result is very interesting.

Madeleine is the daughter of Rosslyn Neave, an antique dealer with a wide range of interests, but who became increasingly fascinated by breadboards. Dedicated boards for bread don't appear to have existed much before 1820. It seems that the Corn Laws drove the price of bread beyond the means of many British families, turning it into a status symbol. And of course, if you can afford bread, you want to let everyone know by showing it off on a lovely hand-carved breadboard.

Early boards were often true luxury items. George Wing of Sheffield produced exquisitely carved boards for the aristocracy, one of which was put up for sale for 16 guineas, roughly equivalent to £2,000 in 2020. These custom-made boards would have been at the heart of the gargantuan breakfasts and teas that characterised genteel country house living for wealthy Victorians.

Naturally, the next step was the breadboard's adoption by the middle classes, and by the 1860s there was a thriving mass market. Decorative themes focused on simple patterns, but the boards get most interesting when amateur carvers make their own boards or personalise them. One board, decorated with ears of wheat and a rose surrounding a shield with monogrammed initials, must have been a wedding gift; another, apparently commissioned for a Rev. Woodfin by a loving congregation, has a quote from Corinthians slap in the middle of it. Many of the boards are deeply worn, and because you're encouraged to handle them, you get an uncanny sense of their history. The museum contains related items such as a trencher, the wooden plate from where we get the word trencherman. There's also a collection of breadknives, which came into being alongside breadboards – after all, if you're showing off your lovely board, you need a lovely knife, right?

Entry to the museum includes a beautifully served cream tea.

05.

Windmill Road, Wimbledon Common, SW19 5NR
Wimbledon tube/train, Putney train or East Putney tube, followed by 93 bus

WIMBLEDON WINDMILL MUSEUM

The daily grind

Wimbledon Common is famous for being home to the Wombles – furry creatures who recycled rubbish in the eponymous 1970s TV series. Like all commons, Wimbledon is land with traditionally shared rights (it's where the word 'commoner' comes from). This common dodged 'enclosure' in 1864 by Earl Spencer, who wanted to develop luxury housing on it – sounds familiar – and has thus preserved its rural feel, including its windmill.

Although there were several watermills on the River Wandle, the local community wanted to produce their own flour. So in 1817, Charles March was granted permission to build the windmill 'upon this condition, that he shall erect, and keep up, a public Corn Mill, for the advantage and convenience of the neighbourhood'. The millers also had to keep watch for duellists, who liked to clash swords on the common.

The mill was closed in 1864 when Earl Spencer decided to build himself a new mansion on the site and fence off Wimbledon Common as his private garden. Understandably, the locals protested. The Earl's plan was shelved by the Wimbledon and Putney Commons Act of 1871, which gave the common back to the people. The mill was converted into living quarters for six families. One of the residents was Lord Baden-Powell, founder of the Boy Scout movement. Today, the windmill has been converted into a small museum. The entrance hall contains the Great Spur Wheel, which used to power it. There are countless models of windmills and interactive displays of working machinery. Kids can get to grips with grinding wheat, lifting sacks of flour, or changing windmill sails. A ladder leads up to the tower where you can see the machinery turning on windy days. The Windmill Museum also contains a small shop, which sells model windmills, honeycomb produced by bees on Wimbledon Common and, of course, Wombles.

ROBERT BADEN-POWELL

06.

50 Mitcham Road, Tooting, SW17 9NA
Tooting Broadway tube

BUZZ BINGO, TOOTING

Chartres Cathedral meets Liberace

Now, alas, a Gala bingo hall, this was the first cinema in the UK to be listed as Grade I – the most rigorous preservation order a building can get. From the outside, the tall, square building doesn't look all that special, give or take a few columns; on the inside, it looks like Chartres Cathedral if it had been designed by Liberace. Opened in 1931, this palace to entertainment was commissioned by Sidney Bernstein, an exiled white Russian who later founded Granada TV, and designed by Fyodor Fyodorovich Kommisarzhevsky, a Russian director and set designer briefly married to actress Peggy Ashcroft.

The heavily gilded foyer is lined with Gothic mirrors and fake leaded windows, punctuated by a pair of sweeping marble staircases. But all this is relatively restrained: the auditorium – inspired by its namesake, the Alhambra Palace in Granada – is where Kommisarzhevsky went bananas. Under a coffered ceiling are cathedral porches, heraldic symbols, and glass chandeliers, now partly obscured by the bingo lighting and screens. The decoration intensifies as you approach the stage. All around the auditorium are arches filled with murals of troubadours and wimpled damsels – but underneath all this medieval madness, the bingo fans play on, eyes fixed on the cards. The combination feels like a weird early version of a themed Vegas casino deep in South London.

In its day, the Granada was the only suburban cinema in London to have its own 20-piece orchestra. The glamorous usherettes wore gold silk blouses with blue slacks, pill box hats, blue cloaks over one shoulder and white gloves, while the doormen wore a blue uniform with brass buttons, peaked caps, and gold epaulettes. On its anniversary, the cinema would serve every customer a slice of cake – wheeled in from the baker next door, it weighed over a ton. Over 2,000 people were turned away on opening night, and over three million viewers came to the pictures here every year. However, the arrival of the television sent audience numbers into a tailspin, and the cinema closed in 1973. It was revived as a bingo hall in 1991.

Frank Sinatra, the Beatles, Little Richard, and the Rolling Stones all played to 3,000 shrieking fans at the Granada, which doubled as a music hall. The original Wurlitzer organ is still here, but its chambers are buried beneath the stage.

07.

Streatham Common South, SW16 3HR
Streatham rail

THE ROOKERY

The beauty of suburbia

It is unlikely that Streatham features in many guide books. Despite spawning a diversity of talents, including supermodel Naomi Campbell, occultist Aleister Crowley (there's something about Streatham High Street that might turn anyone into a Satanist), and William Mildin, 14th Earl of Streatham and allegedly the model for Tarzan, it is an unlovely place. However, in the 18th century, Streatham was a rural haven close to the city, and thus the site of many large country houses.

The Rookery is an area of public gardens adjoining Streatham Common. First opened to the public in 1913, the gardens once belonged to a huge pile of a house that was demolished in the early 1900s. It is an extremely formal garden, quite out of character with the rest of the Common. A series of walks, including a pergola supporting a massive wisteria, radiate out from well-planted central beds. The segmentation of the garden provides ample possibilities for seclusion; this would be a good place for a really serious game of hide-and-seek. The garden slopes down a hill that offers extensive views – admittedly, these include Norbury, but you can't have everything. Other features include a garden with all-white blossoms (and even benches), modelled on Vita Sackville-West's grounds at Sissinghurst, a really good picnic area with fixed tables (very rare in London), and a little covered well in the middle of the garden.

In the summer, the sloping lawns of the Rookery are used to stage performances (a lot of Shakespeare). The park is part of the Capital Ring, a 78-mile walking route around London (tfl.gov.uk/modes/walking/capital-ring) – even if you just do one of the 15 sections, there's plenty to see in each of them.

STREATHAM'S WELLS

The Rookery is laid out above Streatham's original mineral wells, which attracted huge crowds in the 17th and 18th centuries – it was common for coaches full of thirsty punters to queue for a mile along Streatham High Road. Presumably, Queen Victoria didn't have to wait in line when she came to drink her fill. The healing qualities of the waters were first discovered in 1659 when farm hands drank from the spring and experienced its 'purging effects'. This sounds like a reason not to drink the waters, but they were said to cure all manner of ills including rheumatism, gout, jaundice, bilious attacks and blindness.

08.

Sydenham Hill, Crystal Palace Park, SE19 2GA
Penge West or Crystal Palace rail/Overground

CRYSTAL PALACE DINOSAURS

Concrete monsters

One of the strangest pieces of Victoriana extant in London, these life-size concrete dinosaurs were built around a lake in Crystal Palace Park by the sculptor Benjamin Waterhouse Hawkins and unveiled in 1854.

The dinosaurs sparked some controversy at the time. Designed to educate the British public, their anticipation of Darwinism outraged many at a time when creationism rather than evolution was widely accepted. The study of dinosaurs was in its infancy: the word 'dinosaur' was only coined in 1842 by Richard Owen, curator of the Hunterian Museum (see p. 96), who acted as an advisor to Hawkins.

What must then have seemed like a white-hot fusion between art and science now looks a bit silly. The inaccuracy of the models isn't helped by their display, with the animals apparently domesticated around a duck pond. The dinosaurs just look plain weird; although in fairness to Hawkins, working with concrete, lead and iron rods must have been problematic. For many years, the dinosaurs were partially overgrown by the vegetation. Walking around the lake, concrete heads would loom suddenly out of a bush. The installation has since been fully restored, with the original colours re-applied as closely as possible and the addition of two new pterodactyls.

A DINNER PARTY IN THE STOMACH OF AN IGUANODON

The night before the dinosaurs were unveiled, a dinner party was held on 31 December 1853, in the stomach of a half-built Iguanodon. The celebrations began with the toast: 'Saurians and Pterodactyls all! Dream ye ever, in your ancient festivities, of a race to come, dwelling above your tombs... dining on your ghosts'.

Victorian London was in love with the idea of itself as a beacon of enlightenment. Crystal Palace Park on Sydenham Hill embodied this notion. It was purpose-built to re-house the Crystal Palace, centrepiece of the 1851 Great Exhibition in Hyde Park, which was conceived to demonstrate the industrial, military and economic superiority of Great Britain. The park was also where inventor John Logie Baird developed television. After the Crystal Palace burned down in 1936, the park's popularity dwindled, but it remains full of the ghosts of its glorious past. Looming over the athletics stadium is a huge bust of Sir Joseph Paxton, best known for designing the Crystal Palace, and for cultivating the Cavendish banana, the most consumed banana in the western world.

09.

Crystal Palace Parade, SE19 1LG
Crystal Palace rail

CRYSTAL PALACE SUBWAY

Hidden brick beauty

This brickwork jewel of a tunnel is almost all that remains of the High Line station to the Crystal Palace. The Palace, a colossal prefabricated glass and iron structure that housed the Great Exhibition in 1851, was moved from Hyde Park to what was then called Penge Common in 1854. It was the tourist sensation of the day. Visitor numbers were so high that the original Low Line station couldn't keep up with demand. In 1856 the High Line was opened, which shortened the walk to the Palace.

The station was designed by Charles Barry Jr, son of the architect of the Houses of Parliament, and little expense was spared. From the station, first-class passengers entered the subway, which runs under Crystal Palace Parade, now a busy main road, but more of an elegant boulevard in its day. The subway is made up of terracotta and cream brick arches, supported by 15 octagonal columns. It could be a Byzantine crypt rather than a public underpass. Going through a vestibule roofed with glass and iron, visitors would then walk straight into the Palace.

Glory fades, however. In 1936, the Crystal Palace burnt down and the station went into a steep decline. The subway was used as an air raid shelter in the war, with ticketed accommodation for 192 sleepers or 360 standers. After the war, rail traffic ground to a halt and the station fell into disrepair – one local remembers it as being 'very, very creepy'. It finally closed in 1954 and was demolished in 1961, although Ken Russell shot the short film 'Amelia and the Angel' there in 1957.

Only the subway survived. It was used by children as a playground, and in the 1990s for raves, but was eventually sealed for safety reasons. Luckily, it now has supporters – the Friends of Crystal Place Subway – who are working to widen public access and get as much use from the space as possible.

10.

Start at Sydenham Hill station, SE21 7ND
Sydenham Hill rail

SYDENHAM HILL WOODS

Woodland, wildlife, and old masters

This is a good walk. Exit Sydenham Hill station via College Road, cross the road, and head up the broad path to the top of the hill, where the refurbished Dulwich Wood House Inn does very good pub lunches. At the gate, turn left and walk 500 metres along Crescent Hill Road to the upper entrance to Sydenham Hill Woods. The left hand fork descends to the disused line of the High Level railway, built in 1865 to service the Crystal Palace (or Screaming Alice in rhyming slang, if you insist).

Follow the abandoned railway track for a kilometre – diversions in the adjoining woods include seasonal outdoor art installations and a ruined chapel that was once a folly in someone's garden. Eventually, a bench across the path invites you to climb a set of wooden steps leading up to the left. A metal fence separates the woods from a golf course with sweeping city views denied to non-members. Follow the path to an old footbridge, turn left through a metal gate, and descend Cox's Walk to Dulwich Common. Turn left and after a kilometre you will see the stone gates to Dulwich Park. There is a good café in the middle of the park, where you can take your ease. Press on to College Road, where you should stop at the Dulwich Picture Gallery.

You can either walk back up College Road to Sydenham Hill station or turn left up Gallery Road to the entrance of Belair Park, and walk through the park to West Dulwich Station on Thurlow Park Road. This part of London is especially green, a legacy of the swathes of land bought by John Alleyn, a major figure of the Elizabethan theatre and founder of Dulwich College. Alleyn made a couple of very successful marriages, and was proprietor of several profitable playhouses, bear-pits and brothels. The college still owns the land, which has very tight development regulations.

DULWICH PICTURE GALLERY

Built by John Soane, Dulwich Picture Gallery was the first purpose-built gallery in the world. Its solid collection includes works by Poussin, Claude, Rubens, Murillo, Van Dyck, Rembrandt, Watteau and Gainsborough, originally assembled for the King of Poland in 1790 as an 'instant' national collection. When Poland was wiped off the map in 1795 after a series of disastrous wars, the King's collection became available and was eventually housed in Dulwich in 1811.

College Road is named after Dulwich College, one of the country's grander schools. The school motto is 'God's Gift'. Oddly enough, it is the alma mater of Raymond Chandler, author of 'The Maltese Falconand' and 'Farewell, My Lovely'; but it is hard to imagine this as the birthplace of Sam Spade.

11.

100 London Road, Forest Hill, SE23 3PQ
Forest Hill rail

THE HORNIMAN MUSEUM

A balloon with tusks

The Horniman Museum is another creation of a Victorian philanthropist. Opened in 1901, it was commissioned to hold tea merchant Frederick John Horniman's collections of natural history, anthropology, and musical instruments. Like many Victorian collections, what's in the museum looks eccentric because of its apparently random nature. There are some extraordinary objects here, well worth the journey into deepest Forest Hill.

The Horniman's most famous exhibit is probably its stuffed walrus. Taxidermists assembled this from the skin alone, without having any idea of what a walrus actually looked like. Not knowing that the walrus is wrinkled, they stuffed it to the limit, so the finished item looks like a balloon with tusks, and is the size of a small car. Happily, the museum has never corrected this error.

The real jewels of the collection are in the ethnography collection, generally reckoned to be third in importance after the British Museum and the Pitt Rivers collection in Oxford. There is a large amount of fine African statuary – an estimated 22,000 objects, not all of them on display – including systematic collections from the Sua of Zaire and the Hadza of Tanzania.

Best of all is the musical gallery, which was completely renovated between 1999 and 2002. The room is lined with glass cabinets holding instruments from all over the world, and interactive tables allow you to play recordings of any of them. Refurbishment also included the opening of a small aquarium, and converted the entire museum to a more child-friendly format. This means that weekends see herds of haggard, hung-over South London parents with their kids, staring blankly at the fish. Weekdays are probably the best for a serious visit.

Other things to look out for include a stuffed mermaid (the marriage of a dead monkey and a fish by a perverted taxidermist), a glass-walled beehive, and a disconcerting life-size statue of Kali, trampling some very serene heads. The museum café is a bit hit and miss, but the shop is full of quirky little presents. The museum also lays on a very large number of events.

© Cmglee

THE ANALEMMATIC SUNDIAL

The museum is set in 16 acres of gardens with good views across London. The gardens contain an eclectic collection of ten sundials, including a butterfly, a stained-glass window, and an analemmatic sundial, where you can tell the time using your own shadow. So make sure you visit on a sunny day.

12.

45 Melbourne Grove, East Dulwich, SE22 8RG
East Dulwich rail

HOUSE OF DREAMS

Artist in residence

In gentrified East Dulwich, one house stands out from its suburban neighbours. Roses and mosaics frame a bright blue door with a hand-painted sign that reads: 'House of Dreams'. Entering is like tumbling down a rabbit hole into a wonderland of wild colour, a fantastical world made from flotsam and jetsam. Plastic dinosaurs, disembodied dolls, plaster saints and rubber ducks gaze at you from every inch of wall and ceiling. False teeth, bottle tops, tinsel garlands, wigs and watering cans are fashioned into giant sculptures that strike exotic poses. Even the floors are elaborate mosaics made from a kaleidoscope of broken tiles, stained glass and baubles.

Artist in residence Stephen Wright greets visitors with a huge smile and a warm hug. A successful textile, stationery and interior designer, Wright began transforming his home into a work of art in 1998, after developing an interest in outsider art. When his partner and his parents died in quick succession, the work became a form of catharsis. 'It's a sort of shrine made from other people's rubbish,' Wright laughs. 'It's also the diary of my life.' Huge black and white 'memory boards' record moments that have marked Wright's life – some wryly amusing, others searing accounts of bullying and bereavement.

'When my mother died, I discovered safety pins inside all her clothes. Little notes in her handbags. You find all these mysterious secrets about a person you loved after they're gone,' says Wright. 'So I started making sculptures out of my parents' clothes because I wanted to create a family to comfort me.' He obsessively hunts for material in flea markets and junk shops on his frequent travels, from old photographs of strangers to religious votives. The rear garden is filled with plants from his favourite places, a depository of living memories. Increasingly, visitors bring their own memento mori to incorporate into the house – glasses, buttons, ashes, hair.

'By sharing the house with so many people, I want to share the message of freedom of spirit,' Wright explains. 'Our society is becoming more controlled; there are less opportunities for creativity. The House of Dreams is a reaction against that. I want to go back to being a child, where you don't have to explain anything you make. You don't have to follow rules, you can do what you want.'

The house will never be finished. But Wright has bequeathed it to the National Trust, so it will never be lost either.

la librairie éphémère
Atorvastatin 20 mg
UNF

13.

Linden Grove, SE15 3LP
Nunhead rail

NUNHEAD CEMETERY

Gothic nature reserve

Nunhead Cemetery was the second of the seven commercial cemeteries built in a ring around London in the middle of the 19th century to alleviate 'overcrowding' in the graveyards of the City churches. Highgate Cemetery, burial site of Karl Marx – who lived a bourgeois life north of the river in Hampstead – is probably the most famous, but Nunhead, opened in 1840, is possibly the most attractive. Its formal avenues of lime trees still survive, but they enclose a jumble of fallen stone and wilderness. The cemetery covers 52 acres, rising to 60 metres above sea level, thus offering extensive views over the City of London and St Paul's Cathedral between the trees.

In the early 1970s, the United Cemetery Company abandoned Nunhead because a lack of space meant it stopped making money: there was no room for new tenants. After an extensive restoration project the cemetery was reopened in 2001. Now almost completely overgrown, the place is effectively a wildlife reserve, where South Londoners can find songbirds, owls, woodpeckers and around 16 types of butterfly.

The cemetery is typically Victorian, obviously built by a city at the height of its economic power. Wealthy families commissioned mausoleums that are still magnificent today. Of course, like all Victorian developments, the cemetery was a model of efficiency – its circular drive meant that the turnover of services in the chapel could be kept brisk while remaining seemly. The chapel itself has a covered porch for the efficient disembarking of mourners in bad weather; it still stands above a crypt, and looks like a set from a Dracula film. Large monuments, unsettled by root growth, loom out of the trees at strange angles; beseeching stone angels lie surrounded by flowers.

The Friends of Nunhead Cemetery (FONC) offer guided tours starting from the Linden Grove gates at 2pm, usually on the last Sunday of every month. In addition, there are often specialist tours – these might include Music Hall Artistes, Military Connections or a Plant Walk. Monumental inscription recording is carried out by the Friends – volunteers are welcome.

Look for the Scottish Martyrs' obelisk on Dissenters Row, a memorial to five men transported to Australia in 1792 for advocating political reform. The Anglican Chapel designed by Thomas Little in 1843 was recently restored after arson in the 1970s.

14.

1a Carpenter's Place, SW4 7TD
Clapham Common or Clapham North tube

GROWING UNDERGROUND

The world's first subterranean urban farm

Deep below Clapham High Street, 33 metres to be exact, is the world's first subterranean farm. Set up by two friends in 2015, the controlled-environment farm Growing Underground is only accessible by climbing down 193 stairs into an old World War Two air-raid shelter.

Every week, the farm nurtures millions of seeds, seedlings, and green garnishes for sale, similar to hundreds of other farms around the country. Instead of growing its crops across hectares of land, however, this farm grows them 'vertically' on shelves – and it does so without soil, sunlight, or space.

The old air-raid shelter was built in the 1940s with the intention of eventually becoming a south London tube line. The farm setting therefore looks exactly like a tube station, with long narrow rooms and semi-circular ceilings. The building is still owned by Transport for London and you can sometimes hear the tubes from other lines rushing around over the production noises of the farm. The big difference is the cleanliness. Growing Underground is a pristine environment, far away from the mice-infested platforms of the tube. To enter it, you need to don a hair net, sterilised wellies, and lab coat, scrub your hands spotless and then remove all jewellery that could potentially contaminate the herbs.

In the spirit of a Willy Wonka factory, each room is dedicated to a different part of the farming process. The seeds begin their adventure in buckets of oxygenated water where they are cleaned overnight. They are then sprinkled onto recycled carpet cut offs (the substrate replacement for soil) and left for 2-3 days to propagate in a warm, dark room designed to make the plants think they're out in nature, underneath the earth. Once they start sprouting little green shoots they're moved to the farm, where rows and rows of microgreens and salad leaves are left to mature for over a week under the pinky hue of LED lights.

Here is where it gets even more futuristic. Instead of absorbing nutrients from soil, these greens get their goodness from a hydroponic system. Nutrient-infused water is sprinkled over the leaves, which then drips down through to an irrigation system, gets cleaned, re-packed with nutrients, taken back up, and the cycle starts again. It's a water-intense, electricity-heavy system, but the carbon emissions for energy use are claimed to be nil.

The final room is the packaging room where the small herbs and salad garnishes are weighed precisely and sent out to local chefs, shops and supermarkets before ending up on our dinner plates.

15.

Elephant and Castle, SE1 6TG
Elephant & Castle tube/train

MICHAEL FARADAY MEMORIAL

It's a metal box

This … thing, which was previously marooned on a roundabout on the gyratory road system of the Elephant and Castle, has now been enclosed in the pedestrianised area surrounding the shopping centre as the area's redevelopment picks up speed. It's an abandoned disco. It's a storage unit for frozen food. No, in fact, it's a monument to the Victorian scientist Michael Faraday.

The stainless steel box was designed by architect Rodney Gordon in 1959 and built in 1961. The design is not wholly artistic – it contains an electrical substation for the Northern and Bakerloo lines, appropriately enough for a memorial to one of the great pioneers of electricity. It was originally designed to be built of glass to display the workings of the transformer. However, fear of vandalism prevented this, so it was changed to a metal casing. In truth, nothing about the memorial explicitly suggests Faraday, although an inscription in the concrete paving nearby explains that it is his memorial.

The structure aims to stress Faraday's importance as a scientist (Einstein kept a picture of him on his study wall). Born in 1791 in nearby Newington Butts, Faraday came from a poor family and was largely self-taught. Aged 14, he was apprenticed to a bookbinder and spent the next seven years reading at every possible opportunity. In 1831, after years working at the Royal Institution, he discovered electromagnetic induction, the principle behind the electric transformer and generator.

© John Watkins

16.

Bermondsey Walk, SE16 4TT
Bermondsey tube

THAMES PATH CAT

City of cats

This one's for all the cat lovers. London has a surprising number of cat sculptures, from the monstrous black and white mouser looming over Catford market (Catford – you see?) to the small bronze statue of Samuel Johnson's cat Hodge outside the great man's house in Gough Square. Cats crop up throughout the city's past, most famously in the tale of Dick Whittington, a medieval success story who rose from nothing to become mayor of London three times, and who supposedly made his first fortune by selling his cat to a rat-infested country. This iconic London cat has two statues, appearing once curled round the feet of Whittington in front of the Guildhall Art Gallery, and another sat on the Whittington stone at the bottom of Highgate Hill. The Thames Path Cat is a comparatively new addition to this clowder of cats. Part of a group of four statues known as 'Dr Salter's Daydream', the cat lies flat along the Embankment wall, staring at a young girl. They are watched from across the path by a man and a woman, Dr Salter and his wife Ada, who both dedicated their lives to helping the poor of Bermondsey at the end of the 19th century, then one of the roughest and least healthy parts of the capital. Unfortunately, his 8-year-old daughter Joyce contracted scarlet fever, common in deprived areas, and died. This is the little girl who leans smiling against the wall; the cat was her pet, Gorvin. Originally there were just three statues, but in 2014, Ada was added to the group when it was relocated, creating the first public sculpture of a female politician in London – she was London's first female mayor, elected to Bermondsey in 1922. Lean over the wall for a good view up to Tower Bridge, or drop into The Angel pub next door.

THE REMAINS OF EDWARD III'S MOATED MANOR HOUSE

Just south across the road from the statues is a small park that contains the remains of Edward III's moated manor house. All that is left of the building is a low wall, but originally this was a small royal residence built on an island in the river, which the king seems to have used as a base for falconry when he wasn't beating up the French or watching everyone drop dead from the Black Death. The Thames was originally full of islands that have since been absorbed from the river into the city, including Bermondsey and the Isle of Dogs, as well as Thorney Island, where Westminster Abbey now stands.

17.

Ben Pimlott Building, St James's, SE14 6AD
New Cross rail

THE GIANT SCRIBBLE

A squiggle on the skyline

This purpose-built extension of the visual arts department at Goldsmiths College is largely unexceptional: a seven-storey building clad in metal with windows punched through to provide daylight and ventilation for the artists within. But architect Will Alsop has created a landmark in New Cross – one of the least lovely parts of the city – by draping the roof terrace with a giant metal scribble.

British architects tend to be fiends for function over form, but the main purpose of this playful anomaly, highly visible on the South London skyline, seems to be to lift the spirits of travellers driving along the dreary A2. The super-sized scribble has 72 twists and weighs over 25 tonnes. If stretched out, it would be 534m long – over twice as tall as Canary Wharf tower.

The fire escape on the south side, a jagged edge of self-supporting, prefabricated steel, is equally dramatic. The studios at the front of the building are glazed from floor to ceiling, so passers-by can spy on aspiring artists at work. At night, the building is illuminated by industrial lights, creating mysterious pools of light and shadow on the metallic surface.

The alma mater of high-flying British artists such as Damien Hirst, Gillian Wearing, and Anthony Gormley (see p. 216), Goldsmiths College prides itself on a certain edginess, but like the rest of London, the area is starting to see creeping gentrification. Rubbish & Nasty, the clothes and record shop on New Cross Road, is long gone, but the area surrounding the college is still worth exploring.

WILL ALSOP'S LONDON LANDMARKS

Modern architecture in London tends to be associated with Richard Rogers or Norman Foster, so a day spent trailing Will Alsop's playful work would be one well-spent. Most notable are the Peckham Library (122 Peckham Hill Street), an upturned L-shape inspired by an open book, resting on seven wonky columns, and the off-kilter Palestra office block, opposite Southwark tube station. The Blizard Building at Queen Mary University (Turner Street, Whitechapel), wrapped in multicoloured glass and containing moulded pods modelled on giant molecules, is also worth a look.

18.

Court Yard, Eltham, Greenwich, SE9 5NP
Eltham rail, then a half-mile walk or 161 or 126 bus

ELTHAM PALACE

A maximalist's wet dream

A little trouble to get here, but worth the effort, Eltham Palace is one of the most bizarre buildings in London. The original palace was given to King Edward II by Bishop Bek in 1305. King Edward IV added the Great Hall, the only part of the medieval structure still standing. In the 1530s, Henry VIII added royal lodgings and gardens, complete with a bowling green and archery range. It was the only royal palace large enough to contain all Henry VIII's 800 courtiers. The scattered Tudor remains suggest the palace must have been a monster in its prime.

During the 18th and 19th centuries the palace fell into disrepair, but this only heightened its attraction for the Romantic artists of the age and their lust for Gothic ruins. This was a period when wealthy aesthetes actually purpose-built ruins to flit around – lunacy, of course, but popular among the super-rich.

In 1933, the palace was leased by the extravagant socialites Sir Stephen and Lady Virginia Courtauld. The arrival of the Courtaulds (whose relatives founded the famous Courtauld Galleries) marked the palace's renaissance. They instantly ran into controversy by appointing architects Seely and Paget to design a new Art Deco residence incorporating the restored Great Hall. Stately homes in England are too often blighted by an obsession with pseudo-heritage – inglenooks, Palladian bathrooms, half-timbered Tudor garages, and the like. To their credit, the Courtaulds chose a bold, modern design with lashings of English eccentricity.

The exterior of the house is not especially interesting, but the interiors are unexpectedly insane. Dripping with 1930s opulence, the place is a maximalist's wet dream – walls are dressed with exotic veneers and the sunken baths have onyx trimmings. The couple even built a miniature palace filled with jungle murals for their pet ring-tailed lemur, Mah-Jongg, whom they purchased from Harrods. Try to spot the Courtald's yacht moored in the mural of Venice that adorns the entrance hall. The house was also a showcase for the latest technological wizardy: a centralised vacuuming system, synchronised clocks, and concealed ceiling lights.

A circular motif runs riot throughout – domed ceilings, round lights, and portholes. Virginia Courtauld's curved bedroom with a circular ceiling creates the impression of a classical temple. But the snazzy leather map of Eltham in her boudoir bears little resemblance to the Eltham of today, an anonymous suburb of London.

19.

Castle Wood, Shooters Hill, SE18 3RT
North Greenwich tube, then 486 bus, alighting at the Memorial Hospital; or train to Welling rail, then 486 or 89 bus

SEVERNDROOG CASTLE

A folly in the forest

Tucked away in the woods of Shooters Hill, high above South London, sits the folly of Severndroog Castle. Built in 1784 by the widow of naval commander Sir William James, the triangular Gothic-style tower has three rooms sitting on top of one another, with a viewing platform for ten on the roof. On a clear day, you can allegedly see seven counties from the top, although because the platform is high in the treetops, the view can be restricted. But no matter – the tower is built on one of the highest points in London, and the views are spectacular.

The folly was built to commemorate Sir William's life, and in particular his most famous exploit when he destroyed the fleet and fortress of Survarnadurg (hence Severndroog) in India in 1755. According to the British, this was a nest of pirates preying on the East India Company's shipping out of west India; according to the locals, it was the base of the admiral of the Maratha Empire's navy.

Sir William retired to London to work for the East India Company, and died wealthy. The castle passed into private hands, survived a plan to build a 10,000-catacomb cemetery in terraces on the site, and was then used by General William Roy in his trigonometric survey of London, linking the nearby Royal Greenwich Observatory with the Paris Observatory. Next, it served as a lookout for German bombers in both World Wars. It then passed into the hands of the local council, which boarded it up in 1986. After lying derelict for 28 years, it was restored and reopened in 2014.

As well as regular visiting hours, the castle can be privately hired, so check the website before undertaking your journey. There's a tea room on the ground floor.

The castle sits on the Green Chain Walk (tfl.gov.uk/modes/walking/green-chain-walk), a linked system of open spaces between the River Thames and Crystal Palace Park, as well as the Capital Ring, a series of continuous walks beginning in nearby Woolwich. A bit much to do in one day, but a good project if you live here.

Nearby Oxleas Wood contains some of the last remaining ancient woods that once circled the capital. Oxleas Meadow, in the middle of the woods, has a very good traditional British café with views down the hill, across a buried water reservoir and far into Kent.

It was September 1995 and Thomas Jonglez was in Peshawar, the northern Pakistani city 20 kilometres from the tribal zone he was to visit a few days later. It occurred to him that he should record the hidden aspects of his native city, Paris, which he knew so well. During his seven-month trip back home from Beijing, the countries he crossed took in Tibet (entering clandestinely, hidden under blankets in an overnight bus), Iran and Kurdistan. He never took a plane but travelled by boat, train or bus, hitchhiking, cycling, on horseback or on foot, reaching Paris just in time to celebrate Christmas with the family.

On his return, he spent two fantastic years wandering the streets of the capital to gather material for his first "secret guide", written with a friend. For the next seven years he worked in the steel industry until the passion for discovery overtook him. He launched Jonglez Publishing in 2003 and moved to Venice three years later.

In 2013, in search of new adventures, the family left Venice and spent six months travelling to Brazil, via North Korea, Micronesia, the Solomon Islands, Easter Island, Peru and Bolivia.

After seven years in Rio de Janeiro, he now lives in Berlin with his wife and three children.

Jonglez Publishing produces a range of titles in nine languages, released in 40 countries.

Atlas

Atlas of abandoned France
Atlas of extreme weather
Atlas of forbidden places
Atlas of geographical curiosities
Atlas of geographical curiosities - Britain
Atlas of unusual wines

Secret Atlas

New York - The secret atlas
Paris - The secret atlas
Venice - The secret atlas

'Soul of' guides

Soul of Amsterdam
Soul of Athens
Soul of Barcelona
Soul of Berlin
Soul of Brussels
Soul of Detroit
Soul of Kyoto
Soul of Lisbon
Soul of Los Angeles
Soul of Marrakesh
Soul of Marseille
Soul of Milan
Soul of New York
Soul of Paris
Soul of Rome
Soul of Tokyo
Soul of Venice
Soul of Vienna

Photo books

Abandoned America
Abandoned Asylums
Abandoned Australia
Abandoned Belgium
Abandoned Churches: Unclaimed places of worship
Abandoned cinemas of the world
Abandoned France
Abandoned Germany
Abandoned Italy
Abandoned Japan
Abandoned Lebanon
Abandoned Spain
Abandoned USSR
Abandoned world – An AI-generated exploration
After the Final Curtain – The Fall of the American Movie Theater
After the Final Curtain – America's Abandoned Theaters
Baikonur – Vestiges of the Soviet space programme
Cinemas – A French heritage
Clickbait – A visual journey through AIgenerated stories
Forbidden France
Forbidden Places – Vol. 1
Forbidden Places – Vol. 2
Forbidden Places – Vol. 3
Forgotten France
Forgotten Heritage
Oblivion
Parisian Theatres
Secret sacred sites
Venice deserted
Venice from the skies

'Secret' guides

Secret Amsterdam
Secret Bali – An unusual guide
Secret Bangkok
Secret Barcelona
Secret Bath – An unusual guide
Secret Belfast
Secret Berlin
Secret Boston – An unusual guide
Secret Brighton – An unusual guide
Secret Brooklyn – An unusual guide
Secret Brussels
Secret Budapest
Secret Buenos Aires
Secret Campania
Secret Cape Town
Secret Copenhagen
Secret Corsica
Secret Dolomites
Secret Dublin – An unusual guide
Secret Edinburgh – An unusual guide
Secret Florence
Secret French Riviera
Secret Geneva
Secret Glasgow
Secret Granada
Secret Helsinki
Secret Istanbul
Secret Johannesburg
Secret Kuala Lumpur
Secret Lisbon
Secret Liverpool – An unusual guide
Secret London – An unusual guide
Secret London – Unusual bars & restaurants
Secret Los Angeles – An unusual guide
Secret Louisiana – An unusual guide
Secret Madrid
Secret Mexico City
Secret Milan
Secret Montreal – An unusual guide
Secret Naples
Secret New Orleans – An unusual guide
Secret New York – An unusual guide
Secret New York – Curious activities
Secret New York – Hidden bars & restaurants
Secret Normandy
Secret Paris
Secret Potsdam
Secret Prague
Secret Provence
Secret Rio de Janeiro
Secret Rome
Secret Seville
Secret Singapore
Secret Stockholm
Secret Strasbourg
Secret Sussex – An unusual guide
Secret Tokyo
Secret Tuscany
Secret Venice
Secret Vienna
Secret Washington D.C. – An unusual guide
Secret York – An unusual guide

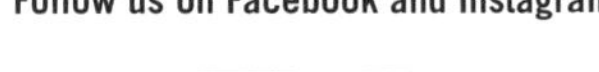

ACKNOWLEDGEMENTS

Our thanks to: Gaby Agis, Etta Lisa Basaldella, Carole Baxter, Frédéric Court, Adam Cumiskey, Nigel Dobinson, Alain Dodard, Benjamin & Maider Faes, Mattie Faint, Patrick Foulis, Ronald Grant, The Greenwich Phantom, Jaco Groot, Charlotte Henwood, John Hilton, Rose Jenkins, Ludovic Joubert, Xavier Lefranc, Islington Local History Centre, Robert Jeffries, Zoe Laughlin, Caoimhe Nic a' Bháird, Alex Parsons-Moore, Valérie Passmore, Clare Patey, David Phillips, Ellis Pike, Jeremy Redhouse, Jane Rollason, Michael van Rooyen, Muffin van Rooyen, avv. Renato Savoia, Chris Slade, Amélie Snyers, Angelos Talentzakis, Boz Temple-Morris, Christopher Wade, David Walter, Harriet Warden, Clem Webb, David White, Shazea Quraishi.

PHOTOGRAPHY CREDITS

Stéphanie Rivoal: Bevis Marks Synagogue, British Optical Association Museum, Bunhill Fields, Doctor Johnson's House, Golden Boy of Pye Corner, The Old Operating Theatre

Jorge Monedero: 2 Willow Road, Alexander Fleming Laboratory Museum, Crystal Palace Dinosaurs, Clown's Gallery & Museum, The Ferryman's Seat, Fetter Lane Moravian Burial Ground, Fan Museum, Buzz Bingo, Tooting, Hunterian Museum, London's First Drinking Fountain, The London Scottish Regimental Museum, Maryleborne Cricket Club Museum, Newgate Cells, New River Walk, Nunhead Cemetery, Princess Caroline Sunken Bath, Ragged School Museum, 'Slice of Reality' and 'Quantum Cloud', Sutton House, Sydenham Hill Woods, Thames River Police Museum, The Cinema Museum, The Coade Stone Caryatids, The Execution Dock, The Executioner's Bell, The Rookery, The Tent, Twining Tea Museum

Peter Scrimshaw: Crossness Pumpig Station

Isobel Akerman (photos and texts): Keystone Crescent, Mounting Block, Myddleton Passage Carvings, Wooden pavement, Timber from a Roman wharf, Fireplace, A miniature St Paul's Cathedral, Bonnington Square Pleasure Garden, Keats Statue, Peek Freans Biscuit Museum, Fossilised Tree stumps, Wanstead Grotto, Herbarium of the Royal Botanic Gardens, Shepherdess Walk Mosaics, Tower Subway, Queen's Silver Jubilee monolith, Roupell street conservation area, Growing Underground, Crossbones graveyard (text and right page photo), Wall of the City of London Corporation car park

Adam Tucker: Crossbones Graveyard (left page photo), Florence Nightingale Museum, Longplayer, London Bridge Model, Marx Memorial Library, Sherlock Holmes Room, Thames Barrier, Tyburn Convent, West London Bowling

Thomas Jonglez: Charnel house at St Bride's, Potsman Park, Royal Exchange ambulatory paintings, Fenton House (right page), Freemason Hall, Cherry tree at the Mitre tavern, Relic of St Etheldreda (left page), Secrets of St Bartholomew's the Greater (left page), Wilton's Music Hall (top and left photo)

The Magic Circle Museum © The Magic Circle - Bleigiessen © Thomas Heatherwick Studio – Auto-icon of Jeremy Bentham © Karmakolle – Grant Museum (top photo) © Grant Museum of Zoology at UCL – Grant Museum (bottom photo) © JRennocks – Crane Park Shot Tower © Marathon – Crystal Palace Subway © James Balton – Dennis Severs house © James Brittain – Eltham Palace © English Heritage Photo Library – God's Own Junkyard © God's Own Junkyard – Horse Hospital © Horse Hospital – Japanese Roof Garden © Brunei Gallery, SOAS University of London – Kirkaldy Testing Museum (right page) © Lars Plougmann – London Wall © Fremantleboy, Drallim – Museum of Brands, Packaging and Advertising © Museum of Brands, Packaging and Advertising – Museum of Curiosities © Oskar Proctor – Severndroog Castle © Severndroog Castle – Sky Garden © Adobe Stock/Pawel Pajor – Tower Bridge Bascule Chamber © Tower Bridge – Two Temple Place © Peter Dazeley – 575 Wandsworth Road © National Trust Images/Cristian Barnett – Secrets of St Batholomew's The Great @ Diliff – London Stone @ GrindtXX – Fenton House (left page) © National Trust Images/Robert Morris – Leighton House © Diego Delso – Horniman Museum (left page) © Nicholas Jackson – Horniman Museum (right page) © Cmglee – John Wesley House © Graham Portlock and Aisha Al-Sadie – Barbican conservatory (right page) © Andy Mabbett – Barbican conservatory (left page) © Henry Kellner – Garden Museum © Rosakoalaglitzereinhorn – Katebet mummy © Gary Todd – London Transport Museum Depot (top photo) © Colin Smith / London Transport – Kingsway tram subway © Tony Hisgett – The relic of St Etheldreada (right page) © Mountain9 – The Queen's Silver Jubilee Monolith © Leo Reynolds – Ascent of the Monument © Diego Delso – Chelsea Physic Garden © Elisa.rolle – Candlelit tours of sir John Soane's Museum © Lewis Bush - Royal Hospital © Steve Cadman – Baps Shri Swaminarayan Mandir (left page) © Meduzanol – Wimbledon Windmill Museum © LegesRomanorum – Michael Faraday Memorial © John Watkins

Maps: **Cyrille Suss** – Layout: **Emmanuelle Willard Toulemonde** – Copy-editing: **Jana Gough and Sigrid Newman** – Proofreading: **Abigail Kafka** – Publishing: **Clémence Mathé**

Cover: **Akhil Pawar – Unsplash**

Registration of copyright: October 2025 – Edition: 01
ISBN: 978-2-36195-969-2
Printed in Italy by L.E.G.O.